STUDY GUIDE
to accompany

INTERNATIONAL ECONOMICS
THIRD EDITION

JAMES GERBER

LAURA A. WOLFF
Southern Illinois University Edwardsville

PEARSON
Addison
Wesley

Boston San Francisco New York
London Toronto Sydney Tokyo Singapore Madrid
Mexico City Munich Paris Cape Town Hong Kong Montreal

Reproduced by Pearson Addison-Wesley from Microsoft® Word files supplied by author.

Copyright © 2005 Pearson Education, Inc.
Publishing as Pearson Addison-Wesley, 75 Arlington Street, Boston, MA 02116

All rights reserved. No part of this publication may be reproduced, stored in a retrieval system, or transmitted, in any form or by any means, electronic, mechanical, photocopying, recording, or otherwise, without the prior written permission of the publisher. Printed in the United States of America.

ISBN   0-321-25670-0

2 3 4 5 6 QEP 07 06 05

Contents

Chapter 1	The United States in a Global Economy	1
Chapter 2	International Economic Institutions Since World War II	7
Chapter 3	Comparative Advantage and the Gains from Trade	17
Chapter 4	Modern Trade Theory	28
Chapter 5	Beyond Comparative Advantage	37
Chapter 6	The Theory of Tariffs and Quotas	46
Chapter 7	Commercial Policy	56
Chapter 8	International Trade and Labor and Environmental Standards	64
Chapter 9	Trade and the Balance of Payments	72
Chapter 10	Exchange Rates and Exchange Rate Systems	85
Chapter 11	An Introduction to Open Economy Macroeconomics	96
Chapter 12	International Financial Crises	105
Chapter 13	Economic Integration in North America	115
Chapter 14	The European Union: Many Markets into One	125
Chapter 15	Trade and Policy Reform in Latin America	135
Chapter 16	Export-Oriented Growth in East Asia	145
Chapter 17	Economic Integration in the Transition Economies	153

Chapter 1
The United States in a Global Economy

■ Vocabulary

For each numbered description, write in the correct term from the list provided.

deep integration gross domestic product (GDP) regional trade agreement
shallow integration index of openness tariff
foreign direct investment (FDI) quota transaction cost

1. A nation's exports plus its imports divided by its GDP, which gives a measurement of how important international trade is to that economy _____

2. Eliminating or reducing trade barriers caused by non-trade-related domestic policies such as labor and environmental standards, rules for fair competition, limits on investment, and government support for specific industries _____

3. Cost of obtaining market information and negotiating and enforcing an agreement _____

4. Agreements between specific groups of nations aimed at either shallow or deep integration among the parties ratifying the agreement _____

5. A tax on internationally traded products _____

6. Reducing the barriers to international goods and services "at the border" by reducing tariffs and quotas _____

7. The market value of all final goods and services produced by an economy in a given time period _____

8. A quantitative restriction on internationally traded products _____

9. Flows of capital representing physical assets such as real estate, factories, and businesses _____

■ Chapter Review

Answer the questions in the space provided below each.

1. International integration of economies is reflected in what three things?
   _____

2. From World War I until the end of World War II, describe three things that happened to world trade.

3. What important technical innovations happened in communication and transportation in the 1800s that promoted global economic integration?

4. What is the most important predictor of the level of investment in a nation?

5. Describe the different types of capital flows. Which is most desired?

6. How do you calculate the index of openness for a nation, and what does this figure tell you about the nation?

7. Name three ways in which global capital markets differ today from those in the late 19th century.

8. What three aspects of international integration today are very different from what existed in 1890?

■ Just the Facts

1. Since World War II, world trade has grown (faster, slower, about the same as) world output. In fact, while world output is _____ times larger, world trade is _____ times larger today than 50 years ago.

2. In the United States about _____ percent of goods and services is produced domestically, which means imports account for _____ percent of U.S. output. In 1890, the United States made about _____ percent of its output domestically, which is not a remarkable change for more than 100 years.

3. In 1950, the ratio of exports to GDP was _____ percent, while in 2000, the ratio was _____. But exports as a percentage of goods production shows a major shift. In 1950 _____ percent of manufactured goods was exported and in 2000 _____ percent was exported. U.S. manufacturers are now far more integrated into the world economy.

4. Trade is a (a larger, a similar, a smaller) share of GDP of most national economies today than in the past.

5. Labor has (more, less, similar) mobility across national boundaries today compared to 1900.

6. At the end of the 19th century, Britain supplied _____ percent of its GDP to world capital markets. Today countries rarely provide more than _____ percent. This supports the claim that global capital flows are not new and have been important for centuries.

7. (Smaller, larger) countries tend to have greater index of openness figures.

8. From 1890 to 1950, the figure for the index of openness for the United States (rose, stayed the same, fell).

9. Most high-income industrialized countries have (low, medium, high) barriers to imports of manufactured goods.

10. Processed foodstuffs, textiles, and apparel are industries that have (no, low, relatively high) barriers to trade in high-income industrialized countries.

■ For Practice

Fill in the missing values for the index of openness in the table below.

The data are from the World Fact Book and are 2002 data in billions of U.S. dollars:

Country	Exports	Imports	GDP	Index of Openness
Finland	40.1 B	31.8 B	133.8 B	—
Netherlands	243.3 B	201.1 B	437.8 B	—
Singapore	127 B	113 B	112.4 B	—
Costa Rica	5.1 B	6.4 B	32 B	—
Ghana	2.2 B	2.8 B	41.25 B	—
Vietnam	16.5 B	16.8 B	183.8 B	—

■ Review Quiz

Check your mastery of the chapter by selecting the letter that gives the correct answer to each question.

1. Volatile capital flows and speculation are features unique to global capital markets in the last 20 years and mark a big change from past centuries.
   (a) True
   (b) False

2. According to your text, which of the following is NOT one of the features of the international governmental organizations (such as the WTO, the IMF, and the World Bank) that deal with global economic issues?
   (a) Serve as forums for discussing and establishing rules
   (b) Mediate disputes
   (c) Organize actions to solve problems
   (d) Have little participation from low-income and lower-income developing countries
   (e) Are controversial

3. The United States has become progressively more open to trade and foreign investment over the years since 1890.
   (a) True
   (b) False

4. How are capital markets today different from capital markets in the late 1800s?
   (a) The problems of speculation and capital flight
   (b) Reacting to changes in technology and communication
   (c) Savings from one nation flowing into another nation
   (d) The need to manage exchange rate risk

5. From 1890 to 1950, there was
   (a) an increase in the percentage of world output that was engaged in world trade.
   (b) an increase in foreign direct investment.
   (c) a decline in the U.S. index of openness.
   (d) a decline in tariffs.

6. Suppose a nation exported $400 million, imported $300 million, and had a GDP of $1000 million. The index of openness for this nation would be
   (a) 0.1 or 10 percent.
   (b) 0.3 or 30 percent.
   (c) 0.4 or 40 percent.
   (d) 0.7 or 70 percent.
   (e) more than 100 percent.

7. Which of the following is TRUE?
   (a) A small nation would have a smaller index of openness than a large nation.
   (b) A nation with a higher index of openness must have lower barriers to trade than a nation that has a lower index of openness.
   (c) Large economies tend to be less dependent on trade than small economies.
   (d) As a very large participant in international trade (measured by total exports and imports), the U.S. has an unusually high index of openness.

8. Statistical comparisons of countries show that
   (a) more open economies grow faster than closed economies.
   (b) consumers pay higher prices for goods and services in countries with low trade barriers.
   (c) total output tends to fall in nations with open economies as production shifts abroad.
   (d) trade is generally bad for a country.

9. The evidence of history suggests that countries that were more open to global economic integration had superior economic performance compared with countries that were more closed.
   (a) True
   (b) False

10. The level of global economic integration at the end of the 20th century
    (a) was completely unique in human history in terms of having such a large amount of global integration.
    (b) represented a return to levels of global integration achieved in the prior century with some differences.
    (c) was unusual because it was made possible by technical innovations in transportation and communication.
    (d) was low compared to the 1950s and the World War II years.

Chapter 1 The United States in a Global Economy

■ Answers to Vocabulary

1. index of openness
2. deep integration
3. transaction cost
4. regional trade agreement
5. tariff
6. shallow integration
7. gross domestic product
8. quota
9. foreign direct investment (FDI)

■ Answers to Chapter Review

1. movement of goods and services, movement of capital and labor, and movement of prices
2. nations cut trade ties, partly for strategic military reasons; nations protected home industries from import competition with high tariffs; total world trade declined dramatically
3. New York lined to London by cable, which shrank gap in interest rates and asset prices; construction of national rail networks; development of stock, bond, and commodity exchanges; steamships and better navigation charts; British Navy suppressed piracy and provided security on high seas.
4. Its national saving rate.
5. Flows of financial capital include stocks, bonds, currencies, and bank accounts. Flows of capital representing physical assets such as real estate, factories, and businesses are called foreign direct investment, and this is the kind of capital flow most nations are eager to attract.
6. Add the nation's exports and imports and divide the total by its GDP. It doesn't tell us much about the nation's trade policies, but it does give some sense of how important trade is to the domestic economy.
7. many more financial instruments available now; more transactions now are about protecting against exchange rate risk, where then the world was on a fixed exchange rate standard; significant reduction in the costs of foreign transactions today.
8. Since tariffs and quotas have been reduced, other trade barriers are becoming more significant; a number of international governmental organizations deal with global economic integration where none existed in 1890; the recent increase in the number of regional trade agreements.

■ Answers to Just the Facts

1. faster; 6; 12
2. 87; 13; 92
3. 3.6; 7.7; 8.9; 41.3
4. a larger

5. less
6. 5–10; 2–3
7. smaller
8. fell
9. low
10. relatively high

■ Answer to For Practice

Country	Exports	Imports	GDP	Index of Openness
Finland	40.1 B	31.8 B	133.8 B	0.54
Netherlands	243.3 B	201.1 B	437.8 B	1.02
Singapore	127 B	113 B	112.4 B	2.14
Costa Rica	5.1 B	6.4 B	32 B	0.36
Ghana	2.2 B	2.8 B	41.25 B	0.12
Vietnam	16.5 B	16.8 B	183.8 B	0.18

■ Answers to Review Quiz

1. B
2. D
3. B
4. D
5. C
6. D
7. C
8. A
9. A
10. B

Chapter 2
International Economic Institutions Since World War II

■ Vocabulary

For each numbered description, write in the correct term from the list provided.

autonomy
Bretton Woods conference
common external tariff
common market
customs union
Doha Development Agenda
economic union
foreign exchange reserves
free riding
free trade area
General Agreement on Tariffs and Trade (GATT)
IMF conditionality
institution
International Monetary Fund (IMF)
lender of last resort
most-favored nation (MFN) status
national treatment
nondiminishable or nonrival
nondiscrimination
nonexcludable
partial trade agreement
public goods
sovereignty
trade bloc or regional trade agreement
trade rounds
Uruguay Round
World Bank
World Trade Organization (WTO)

1. An international governmental organization formed at the end of World War II with the initial focus of reconstruction of war-torn areas that today lends to developing nations to aid in economic development _____

2. A round of trade negotiations that began in 1986 and concluded in 1993 that led to the formation of the World Trade Organization _____

3. A series of agreements on tariff and trade rules that has been very successful in gradually bringing down trade barriers _____

4. Periodic negotiations between participating countries to incrementally reduce trade barriers and change rules _____

5. A new round of trade negotiations that focuses on numerous problems facing developing countries including the highly protected agricultural sectors of rich countries, difficulties with technological standards and intellectual property rights, and rules about dumping and subsidies _____

6. The requirement that foreign goods be treated similarly to the same domestic goods once they enter a nation's markets _____

7. The requirement that all countries participating in a specific agreement be treated equally _____

8. All WTO members must treat each other as well as they treat their most favored trading partner, although somewhat contradictorily the WTO does allow regional trade agreements that give a more preferred status to that subset of WTO member nations _____

9. A nation is not influenced or affected by the policies of other nations _____

10. Formal or informal sets of rules that govern behavior or set constraints, telling us what is permissible, possibly through a formal organization _____

11. National currencies, such as U.S. dollars, Japanese yen, or euros, that are accepted internationally _____

12. Grew out of the General Agreement on Tariffs and Trade and become a formal organization in 1995 with its focus being to reduce trade barriers and to resolve trade disputes _____

13. The normal price mechanism does not work as a way of regulating access _____

14. Consumption by one person does not diminish the ability of another person to consume the product _____

15. A good that is nonexcludable, nonrival, and nondiminishable _____

16. Consumers enjoy the benefits of a product without paying because they cannot be excluded from consumption _____

17. An institution that can help financial intermediaries or governments with loans to prevent temporary financial crises from becoming a full-blown financial collapse _____

18. Two or more countries agree to liberalize trade in a selected group of categories _____

19. The requirement that borrowing nations change their policies so that the economic crisis cannot recur as a condition of taking a loan _____

20. The right of nations to pursue domestic policies that they perceive to be in their national interest and to be free from the intervention of foreign powers in their domestic affairs _____

21. An agreement between nations that allows goods and services from participating countries to cross their international borders free of tariffs and quotas _____

22. An agreement between nations that allows goods and services from participating countries to cross their international borders free of tariffs and quotas and that sets common trade barriers toward all nonmember countries _____

23. An agreement between nations that allows goods and services from participating countries to cross their international borders free of tariffs and quotas; that sets common trade barriers toward all nonmember countries; and that allows for the free movement of factors of production (such as labor and capital) within the participating countries _____

24. An agreement between nations that allows goods and services from participating countries to cross their international borders free of tariffs and quotas; that sets common trade barriers toward all nonmember countries; that allows for the free movement of factors of production (such as labor and capital) within the participating countries; and that creates substantial coordination of macroeconomic policies, including a common currency and harmonization of most standards and regulations
    _____

25. A meeting between U.S., U.K, and other allied nation officials at the end of World War II that led to a series of agreements to create an exchange rate system, the World Bank, and the IMF
    _____

26. Agreements between specific groups of nations aimed at either shallow or deep integration among the parties ratifying the agreement   _____

27. Participating nations agree to treat imports from non-members the same   _____

28. Institution formed at the end of World War II to assist in the maintenance of the exchange rate system
    _____

■ Chapter Review

Answer the questions in the space provided below each.

1. What are the three main global economic organizations that play a major role today in international economic relations? Describe when they were formed and their primary mission.
   _____

2. What is the G–7, and which nations make up its membership?
   _____

3. What significance does Bretton Woods have for international economists?
   _____

4. What are the five types of international economic institutions described in your text?
   _____

5. Describe the conditions that the IMF can place on a borrowing nation.
   _____

6. What is the relationship between GATT and the WTO?
   _____

7. In the late 1990s, WTO trade talks led to opening which sectors?
   _____

8. When were subsidies first addressed in GATT trade talks, and how does a subsidy give firms a competitive advantage?
   _____

9. What powers can an international institutions use against nations that are not cooperating with agreements?

10. What are the four types of regional trade agreements?

11. What is the main difference between a free trade area and a customs union?

12. Forming a common market or an economic union requires more than the reduction of tariffs and quotas. What specifically would participating nations have to agree to do?

13. Regional trade agreements seem to violate the WTO principle of equal treatment (most favored nation). Explain what MFN status is and why the WTO tolerates regional trade agreements.

14. How do international economic institutions contribute to global economic integration?

15. Name three factors that have reduced the autonomy of individual nations.

■ Just the Facts

1. For the IMF, important decisions are made by vote with the weight of each vote proportional to the nation's (population, quota paid to IMF, length of membership).

2. (High-income, middle-income, low-income) nations have a disproportionate share of the votes on key IMF decisions.

3. The United States controls _____ percent of the total votes at the IMF.

4. One indication of the success of GATT is that world trade has grown _____ percent per year over the last 50 years.

5. Prior to the _____ round, GATT negotiations were organized around product by product negotiations.

6. Counting the Doha Round still in progress, there have been _____ rounds of GATT negotiations.

7. International institutions have (more, less, similar) abilities as national governments to enforce rules.

8. Over _____ regional trade agreements are currently operating according to the WTO. Most have come into effect since (1948, 1965, 1990, 2000).

9. Factor mobility is associated with a (free trade area, customs union, common market) type of regional trade agreement.

10. Nations that participate in a (free trade area, customs union, common market, economic union) would share a common currency.

11. A nation that is not affected on influenced by the policies of other nations is considered (sovereign, autonomous) and nations have (more, less, the same amount) of this quality as they did in 1950.

■ Review Quiz

Check your mastery of the chapter by selecting the letter that gives the correct answer to each question.

1. OPEC is an example of which type of international institution?
    (a) Global organization for trade, development, and macroeconomic stability
    (b) International trade agreement involving a few nations
    (c) Development funds and banks
    (d) Commissions and agencies for managing shared resources
    (e) Commodity or industry specific organizations

2. Which of the following does your text classify as a global organization for trade, development, and macroeconomic stability?
    (a) Mekong River Commission
    (b) Inter-American Development Bank
    (c) IMF
    (d) Asia-Pacific Economic Cooperation
    (e) All of the above

3. Which of the following is NOT a member of the G-7?
    (a) Canada
    (b) France
    (c) China
    (d) United States
    (e) Germany

4. Which of the following is NOT a likely problem of a country that lacks foreign exchange reserves?
    (a) It cannot pay for imports.
    (b) It cannot pay its interest payments on its international debt.
    (c) It cannot pay principle payments of its international debt.
    (d) It cannot export products.

5. Which of the following statements about the IMF is false?
    (a) It was formed at the end of World War II.
    (b) It only intervenes in crises by invitation.
    (c) It collects fees from its member nations.
    (d) It provides loans for long run economic development.
    (e) It has more than 180 member nations.

6. Past GATT rounds have addressed
   (a) reducing tariffs.
   (b) dumping.
   (c) subsidies.
   (d) nontariff barriers to trade.
   (e) all of the above

7. Which of the following is false? The Uruguay Round
   (a) began in 1986 and concluded in 1993.
   (b) addressed for the first time trade in services.
   (c) led to the creation of the WTO.
   (d) resolved international trade disputes in the areas of agriculture, textiles, and apparel.

8. The World Bank
   (a) was originally created to assist in the reconstruction of war torn areas.
   (b) has decision making processes largely controlled by low income nations.
   (c) seeks to stabilize private investment flows into developing countries.
   (d) was solely responsible for the rebuilding of Europe after World War II.

9. Since the forming of the WTO, many nations have agreed to open which sector of their economy?
   (a) Telecommunications
   (b) Agriculture
   (c) Textiles
   (d) Apparel
   (e) Pharmaceuticals

10. Which round of trade talks began to address the issue of subsidies?
    (a) Geneva II
    (b) Kennedy
    (c) Uruguay
    (d) Tokyo
    (e) Doha

11. Which of the following is TRUE?
    (a) Tariffs are uniform across countries.
    (b) A goal of GATT has been to create the same tariff for all countries.
    (c) The IMF intercedes by invitation when a nation has an international payments crisis.
    (d) Everyone agrees that the work of the IMF, World Bank, and WTO has been positive for the global community.

12. Which of the following is NOT addressed in the Doha Development Agenda?
    (a) Highly protected agricultural markets in rich countries
    (b) Difficulty many low-income countries have in implementing technical standards and intellectual property rights protection
    (c) Rules governing dumping and subsidies
    (d) Reduction of quotas on manufactured products

13. Which of the following would be an example of a partial trade agreement? Two or more countries agree to
    (a) allow goods and services to flow across their borders without tariffs or quotas.
    (b) allow workers and capital to move within their region without limitations.
    (c) reduce tariffs on semiconductors.
    (d) adopt a common currency and create a regional central bank to make monetary policy decisions.

14. To go from a free trade area to a customs union, participating nations would have to agree to
    (a) adopt a common currency.
    (b) substantially coordinate their fiscal and monetary policies.
    (c) allow the free movement of labor and capital across borders.
    (d) create common trade barriers toward nonmember nations.

15. Which type of agreement represents the shallowest level of economic integration?
    (a) Free trade area
    (b) Customs union
    (c) Common market
    (d) Economic union

16. In today's world, all nations are less autonomous than they were in the past.
    (a) True
    (b) False

17. Which of the following is FALSE about the international economic institutions?
    (a) They have generally done a good job of building support for open markets.
    (b) They have brought more efficiency to international economic policies.
    (c) They have effectively addressed the inequalities of income and opportunity that exist throughout the world.
    (d) They helped overcome free rider problems in the provision of international public goods, such as a lender of last resort and the gradual, coordinated reduction of trade barriers.

■ Answers to Vocabulary

1. World Bank
2. Uruguay Round
3. General Agreement on Tariffs and Trade (GATT)
4. trade rounds
5. Doha Development Agenda
6. national treatment
7. nondiscrimination
8. most-favored nation (MFN) status
9. autonomy

10. institution
11. foreign exchange reserves
12. World Trade Organization (WTO)
13. nonexcludable
14. nondimisishable or nonrival
15. public good
16. free riding
17. lender of last resort
18. partial trade agreement
19. IMF conditionality
20. sovereignty
21. free trade area
22. customs union
23. common market
24. economic union
25. Bretton Woods conference
26. trade bloc or regional trade agreement
27. common external tariff
28. International Monetary Fund (IMF)

■ Answers to Chapter Review

1. The World Bank was formed at the end of World War II with its main mission the reconstruction of war torn areas, which was later expanded to include the economic development of low-income nations. The International Monetary Fund (IMF) was formed at the end of World War II to assist in the maintenance of the exchange rate system, and later to focus on assisting nations experiencing economic crises. The World Trade Organization (WTO) was formed in 1994 as a global institution to promote freer trade and to resolve trade disputes.

2. The seven largest industrial economies, which include Canada, Italy, France, Germany, Japan, the United States, and the United Kingdom

3. This meeting at the end of World War II led to the formation of the IMF and the World Bank. The need for an institution to address trade disputes and to reduce trade barriers was also recognized.

4. Commodity or industry specific organizations, Commissions and agencies for managing shared resources, Development funds and banks, International trade agreement involving a few nations, Global organization for trade, development, and macroeconomic stability

5. In addition to the interest it charges on loans, the IMF can require borrowing nations to change their policies so the problems do not recur. This could include simple economic reforms or more fundamental changes in the relationship between the government and the market.

6. GATT was a series of trade negotiations and agreements that ultimately led to the creation of the World Trade Organization in the agreement known as the Uruguay Round.

7. telecommunications, financial services

8. The Tokyo Round. With a subsidy, the national government pays part of the firm's production costs directly or indirectly, possibly through subsidized interest rates or artificially cheap access to foreign currency.

9. Their powers are subtle, but include the ability to withdraw support or access to programs and to legitimize retaliatory sanctions. They rely mainly on moral suasion, and it ultimately requires individual nations to keep their commitments,

10. free trade area, customs union, common market, and economic union

11. A free trade area allows goods and services to cross the participating countries' borders without tariffs or quotas, but does not require the nations to change their trade policies toward non-member nations. A customs union requires the participating nations to negotiate common external barriers to trade, meaning each will treat imports from non-member countries the same.

12. With a common market, factor mobility is introduced. Labor and capital are free to cross borders. With an economic union, substantial coordination of macroeconomic policies is required, including a common currency and harmonization of standards and regulations.

13. MFN status is basically that you will treat all nations participating in the agreement the same. A regional trade agreement creates preferential treatment for nations that are participants. (For example, because of NAFTA, Mexico and Canada get more preferential terms with the United States than other WTO members would.) The WTO recognizes that regional agreements destroy some opportunities for trade (by making nonmembers face higher barriers than members), but believes they create more trade between participants than they destroy. The regional agreements also allow nations to try out new arrangements that may later be adopted more broadly.

14. increased stability, reduced uncertainty

15. The deepening of trade relations, the growth of migratory flows of people across international boundaries, and the emergence of internationally accessible capital markets.

■ Answers to Just the Facts

1. quota paid to IMF
2. High-income
3. 17
4. 6
5. Kennedy
6. 9
7. less
8. 184, 1990
9. common market
10. economic union
11. autonomous, less

■ Answers to Review Quiz

1. E
2. C
3. C
4. D
5. D
6. E
7. D
8. A
9. A
10. D
11. C
12. D
13. C
14. D
15. A
16. A
17. C

Chapter 3
Comparative Advantage and the Gains from Trade

■ Vocabulary

For each numbered description, write in the correct term from the list provided.

absolute productivity advantage
autarky
comparative productivity advantage
competitive advantage
economic restructuring
gains from trade
labor productivity
mercantilism
opportunity cost
price line or trade line
production possibilities curve (PPC)
relative price
trade adjustment assistance (TAA)
zero sum

1. The improvement in national welfare from engaging in trade _____

2. A system on nationalistic economics that dominated economic thought in the 1700s
_____

3. One nation's gain is another nation's loss _____

4. Units of output divided by the number of hours worked _____

5. Being able to produce more output per hour worked compared to a trading partner
_____

6. How much of an alternate product a producer must give up in order to produce one unit of this product _____

7. A curve that indicates the various combinations of two products that could be produced from a given set of resources and that illustrates the trade offs a nation faces as it chooses which combination to produce _____

8. Another name for the opportunity cost or the trade off involved in producing a unit of output
_____

9. The complete absence of trade _____

10. A line that illustrates the trading possibilities for a nation _____

11. Being able to produce a product at a lower opportunity cost than a trading partner
_____

12. Being able to sell product at a lower market price than a trading partner, perhaps because the product's price does not accurately reflect input costs due to government subsidies or externalities
_____

13. Changes in the economy that require some industries to grow while others shrink or perhaps disappear _____

14. A situation where winners from trade compensate losers, usually through some sort of government program offering extended unemployment benefits, worker retraining, and perhaps temporary restrictions on sudden surges in imports. _____

■ Chapter Review

Answer the questions in the space provided below each.

1. Adam Smith initiated an attack on mercantilism in his book, *An Inquiry into the Nature and Causes of the Wealth of Nations*. What did mercantilists believe about trade?

2. What did Adam Smith perceive as the source of the many improvements in the standard of living that occurred in his lifetime, and what important insight did he contribute to economic theory regarding this?

3. Describe the basic assumptions of the simple trade model presented in the chapter.

4. Define productivity and describe how you would calculate it for labor in the simple model.

5. How can a country be more productive than a trading partner and still gain from trade with that partner? Use the concepts of absolute advantage and comparative advantage in your answer.

6. Why might there be a difference between comparative advantage and competitive advantage? If there is a difference, what is the result for a nation that pursues competitive advantage rather than comparative advantage?

7. If free trade leads to economic restructuring, why might it be controversial, even if it is good for the nation as a whole?

8. Trade adjustment assistance is common in many countries. What justifications do proponents offer for these programs?

Chapter 3 Comparative Advantage and the Gains from Trade   19

■ Just the Facts

1. _____ first created the simple trade model presented in the chapter.

2. The volume of trade in _____ exceeds the volume of trade of any other good or service other than currency trading.

3. In 2002, _____ was the top supplier of oil to the United States, but more than _____ percent of the oil the United States imported came from the Western Hemisphere.

4. Absolute advantage is based on differences in (productivity, opportunity cost, wages).

5. Comparative advantage is based on differences in (productivity, opportunity cost, wages).

6. Suppose Canada can produce 4 loaves of bread per hour worked or 1 unit of timber. If the U.S. can produce 6 loaves of bread or 3 units of timber, the relative price of bread in Canada will be (higher than, lower than, the same as) the relative price of bread in the United States. Canada should produce (bread, timber). The countries would trade bread for timber at a ratio somewhere between _____ bread for a unit of timber and _____ bread for a unit of timber.

7. The slope of a nation's production possibilities curve is also the _____ price or opportunity cost of producing the product on the horizontal axis. To get the opportunity cost of the product on the vertical axis, calculate the _____ of the slope of the production possibilities curve.

8. If the domestic price is below the trade price, the good will be _____.

9. In the simple model, nations (completely, partially, do not) specialize in the production of the product in which they have a comparative advantage.

10. Since the passage of NAFTA, U.S. and Canadian exports of autos to Mexico have (increased, decreased, remained the same).

■ For Practice

Calculate the answers for the problems below.

1. Use the information given in the table below to answer questions (a)–(e).

   Suppose each nation can produce the following amount of output per hour worked.

	China	Japan
Shirts	12	16
Tractors	2	4

(a) Which nation has an absolute productivity advantage in tractor production?
(b) Which nation has an absolute productivity advantage in shirt production?
(c) Which nation has a comparative advantage in tractor production?
(d) Which nation has a comparative advantage in shirt production?
(e) Draw each nation's production possibilities curve on the graphs below. Assume each nation specializes completely in the production of the product in which it has a comparative advantage. Draw a possible post trade price line/trade line for each nation.

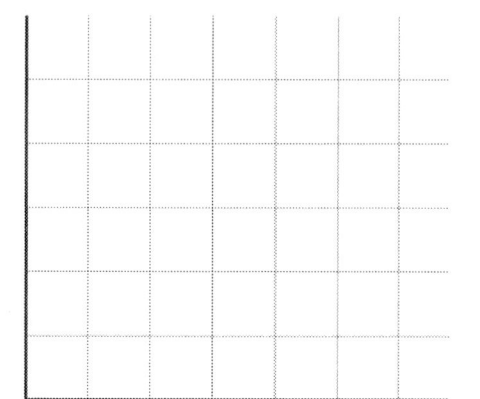

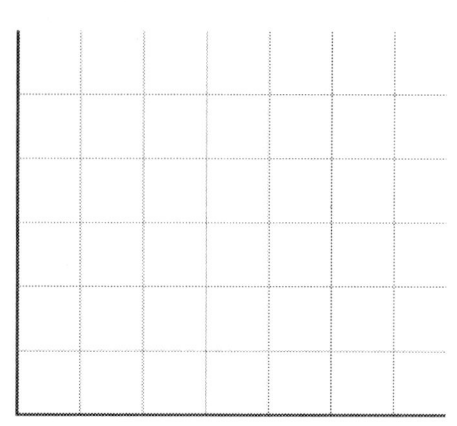

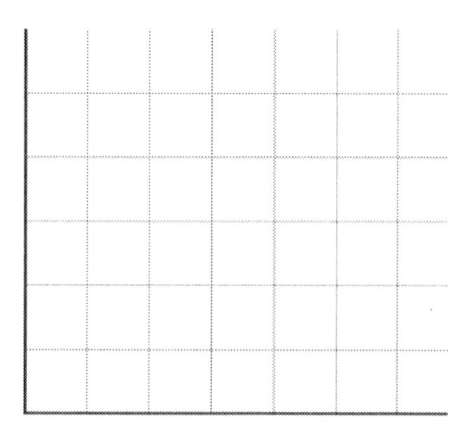

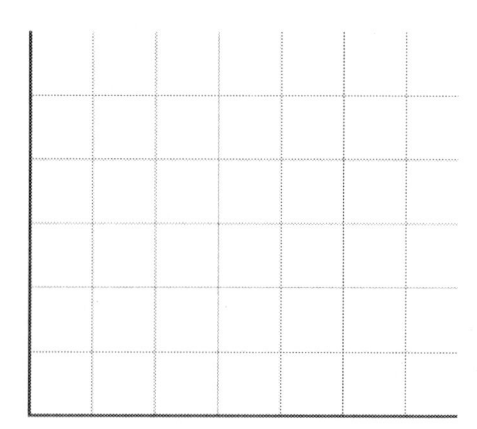

2. Use the information given in the table below to answer questions (a)–(e).

   Suppose each nation can produce the following amount of output per hour worked.

	Ghana	Kenya
Cotton	9	8
Generators	3	8

   (a) Which nation has an absolute productivity advantage in generator production?
   (b) Which nation has an absolute productivity advantage in cotton production?
   (c) Which nation has a comparative advantage in generator production?
   (d) Which nation has a comparative advantage in cotton production?
   (e) Draw each nation's production possibilities curve on the graphs below. Assume each nation specializes completely in the production of the product in which it has a comparative advantage. Draw a possible post trade price line/trade line for each nation.

3. Use the information given in the table below to answer questions (a)–(e).

Suppose each nation can produce the following amount of output per hour worked.

	Costa Rica	**Guatemala**
Coffee	20	14
Computers	4	2

(a) Which nation has an absolute productivity advantage in coffee production?
(b) Which nation has an absolute productivity advantage in computer production?
(c) Which nation has a comparative advantage in coffee production?
(d) Which nation has a comparative advantage in computer production?
(e) Draw each nation's production possibilities curve on the graphs below. Assume each nation specializes completely in the production of the product in which it has a comparative advantage. Draw a possible post trade price line/trade line for each nation.

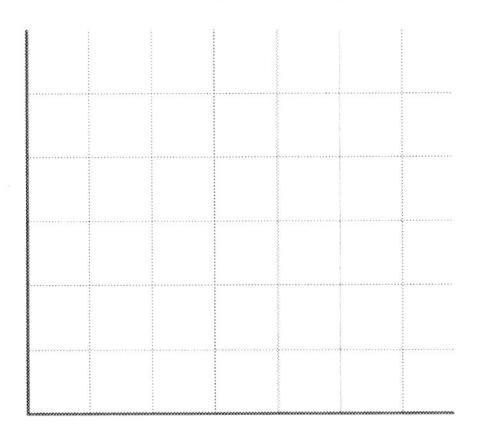

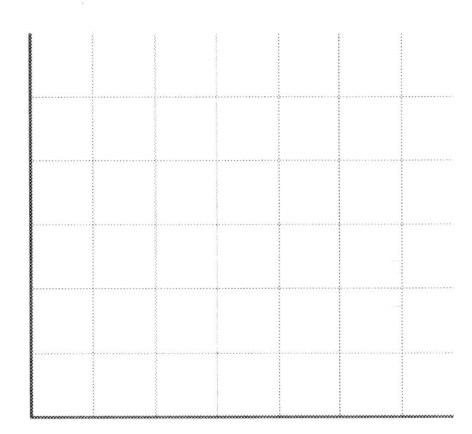

■ Review Quiz

Check your mastery of the chapter by selecting the letter that gives the correct answer to each question.

1. Which of the following is FALSE?
   (a) Adam Smith believed that every nation would have an absolute advantage in something.
   (b) David Ricardo's model emphasizes comparative advantage as the basis for the gains from trade.
   (c) High-income countries cannot gain from trade with low-income countries, unless the low-income country has an absolute advantage in some product due to climate or other resources
   (d) Gains from trade do not depend on having an absolute advantage.

2. Which of the following is TRUE?
   (a) Comparative advantage in crude oil production depends largely on labor costs.
   (b) If a country does not buy oil from the Middle East, it will not be affected by a disruption in Middle East oil supplies.
   (c) The Middle East has less than 50 percent of the world's proven crude oil reserves.
   (d) At current prices, most of the world's oil reserves is too expensive to recover and market.

3. If market prices do not accurately reflect the economic value of an input or an output, a firm's
   (a) comparative advantage will equal its competitive advantage.
   (b) comparative advantage will equal its absolute advantage.
   (c) competitive advantage will equal its absolute advantage.
   (d) competitive advantage may not equal its comparative advantage.

4. Which of the following is TRUE?
   (a) Policies that make individual firms highly profitable through trade barriers often make the nation's overall standard of living lower.
   (b) Policies that create competitive advantages where the firms lack comparative advantage improve national welfare.
   (c) Policies that are good for individual firms or industries in a country are always also good for the nation as a whole.
   (d) One nation's growth is always at the expense of another nation.

5. If a nation follows commercial policies that create competitive advantages for its firms where no comparative advantage exists,
   (a) the nation will enhance living standards for its citizens.
   (b) the nation will improve resource allocation.
   (c) the nation will maximize the value of national output.
   (d) the nation will have a lower value for national welfare.

6. The availability of foreign made goods does all of the following EXCEPT
   (a) increases our choices as consumers.
   (b) lowers the cost of inputs to producers.
   (c) allows us to achieve smaller but more varied bundles of overall consumption goods.
   (d) increases competition and innovation.
   (e) leads to a diffusion of technological change.

7. Why are wages in developing countries lower?
   (a) Workers in developing countries produce more output per hour than workers in industrialized countries.
   (b) Workers in developing countries have more skill than workers in industrialized countries.
   (c) Workers in developing countries have less access to capital both on the job and in the surrounding community to support the economy than would workers in industrialized countries.
   (d) Workers in developing countries have higher productivity than workers in industrialized countries.

8. Suppose France can produce 3 units of wine with one hour of labor or 1 pair of shoes. Suppose Italy can produce 2 units of wine with one hour of labor or 2 pairs of shoes. Which of the following statements is TRUE?
   (a) France has an absolute advantage in shoes.
   (b) Italy has an absolute advantage in wine.
   (c) France and Italy cannot gain from trade.
   (d) Italy has a comparative advantage in wine.
   (e) France has a comparative advantage in wine.

9. Suppose Mexico can produce 10 units of oil with one hour of labor or 2 cars. Suppose Canada can produce 12 units of oil or 4 cars. Which of the following statements is FALSE?
   (a) Canada cannot gain from trade with Mexico.
   (b) Canada has an absolute advantage in both oil and car production.
   (c) Canada has a comparative advantage in car production.
   (d) Mexico has a comparative advantage in oil production.
   (e) Canada is more productive at producing both cars and oil than Mexico.

10. Which of the following is a false statement about the U.S. and Mexican auto industries?
    (a) It takes more hours of labor to assemble a car in Mexico.
    (b) U.S. labor costs are much higher than in Mexico.
    (c) Shipping is less expensive in Mexico than it is in the United States.
    (d) Mexican workers have less capital available at work and in the surrounding community than in the United States.

■ Answers to Vocabulary

1. gains from trade
2. mercantilism
3. zero sum
4. labor productivity
5. absolute productivity advantage
6. opportunity cost
7. production possibilities curve (PPC)
8. relative price
9. autarky
10. price line or trade line
11. comparative productivity advantage
12. competitive advantage
13. economic restructuring
14. trade adjustment assistance (TAA)

■ Answers to Chapter Review

1. Mercantilists stressed exports over imports. They emphasized the need to raise revenue to build armies and complete national construction projects. They perceived trade as a zero sum game, where one party wins and the other party loses.

2. Smith observed increasing specialization in production was responsible for increased output and that specialization depends on the size of the market.

3. There are two countries producing two products from the single input of labor. The markets are competitive and firms have no market power. There are no changes in technology and no changes in productivity over time. Labor is mobile between industries within a nation but not between countries.

4. Productivity is the amount of output obtained from a unit of input. For this model, simply divide the units of output by hours worked to get labor productivity.

5. The gains from trade don't rely on overall productivity (absolute advantage) but on differences in relative prices (comparative advantage). In producing a good or service, as long as a trading partner gives up fewer units of an alternate product, we can gain from trade with them.

6. Government policies or mispriced inputs or outputs may lead to a difference between comparative advantage and competitive advantage. A country that creates competitive advantages where there are not comparative advantages misallocates its resources and has lower national well being, although the firms involved may prosper as a result of the misallocation.

7. The nation as a whole is better off as long as the gains from the winners exceed the losses from the losers. Restructuring means that some industries are dying and workers and producers have to find other opportunities. This may be difficult for not only those directly involved in the industry, but also for the surrounding communities.

8. First, the nation as a whole benefits from trade, so there are newly added resources that can be used for compensation. Second, there is a potential ethical obligation to assist those hurt by economic change. Third, compensation reduces the incentives for those hurt by trade to fight against free trade policies.

■ Answers to Just the Facts

1. David Ricardo
2. crude oil
3. Saudi Arabia; 50
4. productivity
5. opportunity cost
6. lower than; bread; 2; 4
7. relative; the inverse
8. exported
9. completely
10. increased

■ Answers to For Practice

1. (a) Japan
   (b) Japan
   (c) Japan because 1 tractor costs 4 shirts, which is lower than China's opportunity cost of 6 shirts.
   (d) China because 1 shirt costs 0.167 tractors, which is lower than Japan's opportunity cost of 0.25 tractors.
   (e)

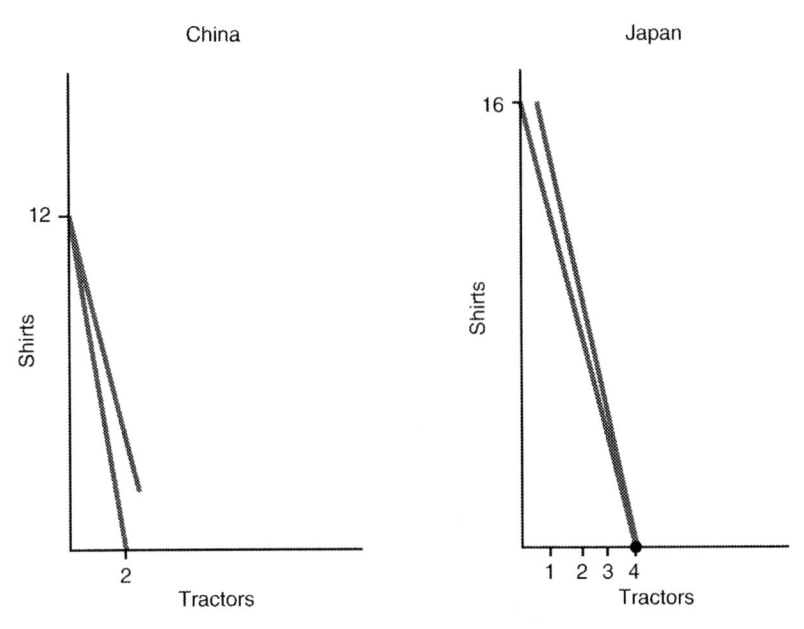

   Possible trade ratio 1 tractor = 5 shirts

2. (a) Kenya
   (b) Ghana
   (c) Kenya because 1 generator costs 1 cotton, which is lower than Ghana's opportunity cost of 3 cotton.
   (d) Ghana because 1 cotton costs 0.33 generators, which is lower than Kenya's opportunity cost of 1 generator.

(e)

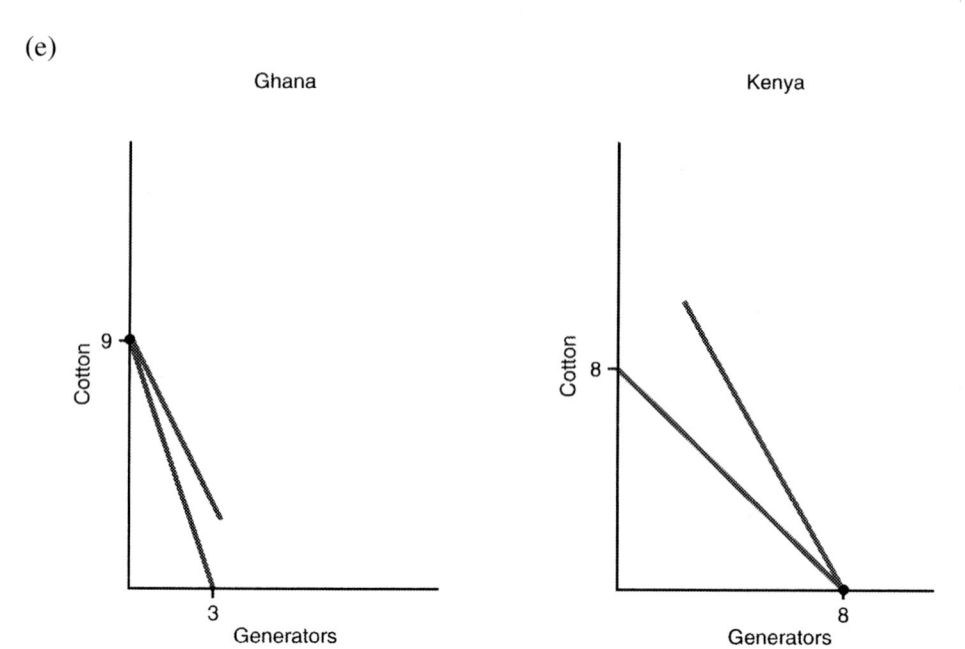

Ghana | Kenya

Possible trade ratio 1 generator = 2 cotton

3. (a) Costa Rica
   (b) Costa Rica
   (c) Guatemala because 1 coffee costs 0.143 computers, which is lower than Costa Rica's opportunity cost of 0.2 computers.
   (d) Costa Rica because 1 computer costs 5 coffee, which is lower than Guatemala's opportunity cost of 7 coffee.
   (e)

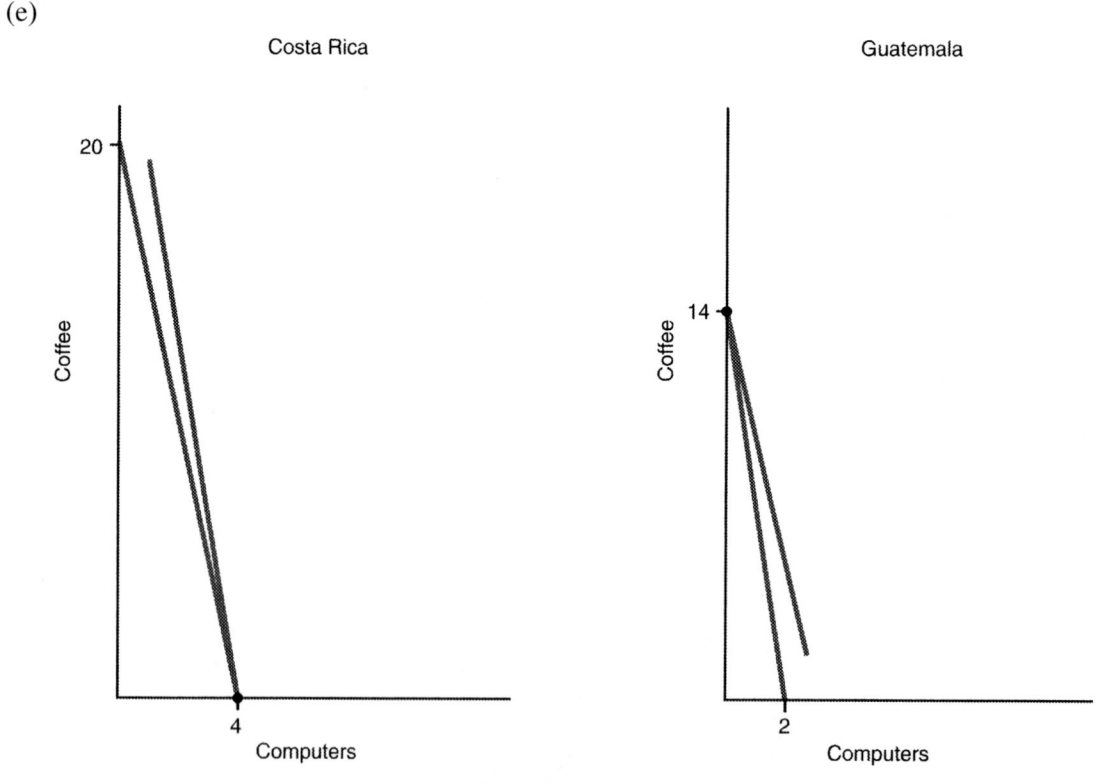

Costa Rica | Guatemala

Possible ratio 1 computer = 6 coffee

Chapter 3   Comparative Advantage and the Gains from Trade   27

■ Answers to Review Quiz

1. C
2. D
3. D
4. A
5. D
6. C
7. C
8. E
9. A
10. C

Chapter 4
Modern Trade Theory

■ **Vocabulary**

For each numbered description, write in the correct term from the list provided.

derived demand intra-firm trade product cycle
factor abundance magnification effect specific factors model
factor scarcity OLI theory Stolper-Samuelson theorem
Heckscher-Ohlin (HO) trade theory

1. Given a ratio of two factors of production, such as labor and capital, a nation has a higher ratio of one of the factors of production compared to a trading partner _____

2. Given a ratio of two factors of production, such as labor and capital, a nation has a lower ratio of one of the factors of production compared to a trading partner _____

3. A country's comparative advantage lies in the production of goods that require more intensively its relatively abundant factors of production _____

4. A situation where the demand for one item depends on the demand for something else _____

5. An increase in the price of a product raises the income earned by the factors of production that are used intensively in its production _____

6. A change in the price of the output causes a much greater change in factor incomes _____

7. A product requires a unique factor of production, which is immobile, meaning it can't easily be switched to the production of alternate products _____

8. As a manufactured product evolves technologically, the types of factors of production required to produce it changes _____

9. International trade between a parent company and a foreign-owned affiliate _____

10. An eclectic theory of foreign direct investment combining both macroeconomic and microeconomic elements _____

Chapter 4 Modern Trade Theory

■ Chapter Review

Answer the questions in the space provided below each.

1. What did Adam Smith and David Ricardo believe would determine each nation's relative productivity?

2. What variable have several modern economists identified as a potential source of comparative advantage?

3. What observations does the Heckscher-Ohlin model make about the differences between nations and between products?

4. State the Heckscher-Ohlin theorem.

5. Compare and contrast the assumptions of the Ricardian simple trade model from Chapter 3 with the Heckscher-Ohlin model.

6. Why don't nations completely specialize in the production of the product in which they have a comparative advantage in the Heckscher-Ohlin model?

7. Explain the effects on income of capital owners and on labor owners in a capital abundant country once trade is introduced.

8. Describe the magnification effect.

9. What does your text identify as the key determinant of trade's effect on the income of factors of production?

10. Suppose beer requires the specific factor of capital, olives require the specific factor of land, and labor is variable. If Belgium is capital abundant and Portugal is land abundant, describe the effects on income distribution after trade begins.

11. What have been the problems with empirical tests of comparative advantage?

12. Describe the product cycle model of trade.

13. What inputs are needed in the early phase of the product cycle?

14. What happens to the product cycle as it leaves the early phase?

15. Is the product cycle model a contradiction of comparative advantage based trade models? Why?

16. How might the product cycle lead to intra-firm trade?

17. According to the case study on NAFTA, which U.S. industries were expected to do well and which were expected to do poorly as a result of the trade agreement?

18. According to OLI theory, what factors might make a company more likely to invest abroad than to export?

19. According to the case study on U.S.–China trade, which Chinese exports can be explained by the product cycle?

20. Which types of workers are most likely to favor lowering trade barriers?

■ Just the Facts

1. Suppose India and China have similar amounts of labor, but China has twice as much capital as India. This means that (China, India, neither nation) is the capital abundant country and (China, India, neither nation) is the labor abundant country.

2. Examples from the text of products that the United States has a comparative advantage in based on its factors of production include _____ and _____.

3. In the Ricardian simple trade model, opportunity costs were _____. In the Heckscher-Ohlin model, opportunity costs are _____.

4. In the HO model, as additional units of one product are produced, the nation must give up (fewer units, the same amount of units, more units) of the alternate product.

5. If there is an increase in the demand for computers, there will be (an increase, no change, a decrease) in demand for the inputs used to produce computers. Those resources that are particularly required for computer production will have their incomes (rise, fall, be unchanged).

6. According to the magnification effect, a percentage change in the price of an output will cause a (larger, smaller, similar) percentage change in the price of the input used intensively in its production.

7. _____ created the product cycle model of trade.

8. Marketing and consumer feedback is most important in the (early, middle, late) phase of the product cycle.

9. _____ created the OLI theory of foreign direct investment.

10. The O in OLI theory stands for _____.

11. The L in OLI theory stands for _____.

12. The I in OLI theory stands for _____.

13. Since the 1960s, manufacturing in North America and Europe has (increased, decreased, remained about the same) when measured as a share of GDP and as a share of overall employment.

14. Wage inequality has (increased, decreased, been unchanged) in the United States over the last 30 years. This has particularly negatively affected workers that are _____ or that have _____.

15. A majority of the reductions in manufacturing employment in all industrial countries appears to have resulted from _____.

16. As skilled labor has become more expensive over the last two decades, firms have used _____ skilled labor in industrialized countries and as unskilled labor has become cheaper, firms have used _____ unskilled labor. This seems to be primarily due to changes in _____.

■ For Practice

1. Use the following information to answer questions (a)–(f).

	South Africa	Nigeria
Capital	100 machines	25 machines
Labor	200 workers	100 workers

    (a) What is South Africa's capital to labor ratio?
    (b) What is Nigeria's capital to labor ratio?
    (c) Which nation is capital abundant?
    (d) Which nation is labor abundant?
    (e) Suppose apparel requires a lower capital to labor ratio and mining requires a higher capital to labor ratio. South Africa will have a comparative advantage in which product?
    (f) In Nigeria, the owners of which factor of production will see their incomes rise after trade begins with South Africa?

2. Use the following information to answer questions (a)–(f).
    Assume the following values for the variables listed below.

    $$K_{Brazil} = 20$$
    $$K_{Peru} = 12$$
    $$L_{Brazil} = 80$$
    $$L_{Peru} = 72$$

Suppose further that production requirements for orange juice and for potatoes are such that:
$K_{orange\ juice}/L_{orange\ juice} > K_{potatoes}/L_{potatoes}$

(a) Calculate the value for K_{Brazil}/L_{Brazil}
(b) Calculate the value for K_{Peru}/L_{Peru}
(c) Which country is capital abundant?
(d) Which country is labor abundant?
(e) Which country will produce more orange juice after trade begins?
(f) In Peru, which resource owners will have higher incomes because of trade?

■ Review Quiz

Check your mastery of the chapter by selecting the letter that gives the correct answer to each question.

1. Suppose Argentina is land abundant and that beef is particularly intensive in its use of land. Suppose Chile is capital abundant and mining is particularly intensive in its use of capital. According to the chapter,
   (a) Argentina will have more mining enterprises after trade begins.
   (b) land owners in Argentina will have lower incomes after trade begins.
   (c) capital owners in Chile will be opposed to trade with Argentina.
   (d) land owners in Argentina will be supporters of free trade with Chile.

2. Suppose Finland has 70 units of capital and 10 units of labor. Suppose Russia has 50 units of capital and 150 units of labor. Which of the following is false?
   (a) Finland is capital abundant compared to Russia.
   (b) Russia is labor abundant compared to Finland.
   (c) If free trade opens between Finland and Russia, Russian capital owners will likely see a decrease in their income.
   (d) Workers in Finland would likely favor free trade with Russia.

3. Suppose $(K/L)_{vegetable\ oil} > (K/L)_{strawberries}$. If $(K/L)_{Spain} < (K/L)_{France}$, then
   (a) Spain will produce vegetable oil.
   (b) labor in France will have higher incomes once trade with Spain is introduced.
   (c) capital owners in Spain will likely favor trade barriers against French imports.
   (d) labor in Spain will have lower incomes once trade with France is introduced.

4. Which of the following is false? When trade opens,
   (a) each country follows its comparative advantage and moves toward greater specialization.
   (b) the shift in production alters the demand for specific factors.
   (c) the specific factor in the expanding industry experiences a decrease in its income.
   (d) in the long run, specific factors may move between output sectors.

5. Empirical tests of the theory of comparative advantage
   (a) have universally proven it to be accurate in predicting real world trade flows.
   (b) are very simple to conduct.
   (c) have been more successful for Ricardian trade models than for HO models.
   (d) have not had measurement problems with data on factor endowments.

6. Trade
   (a) causes some firms to shut down.
   (b) leads to more overall jobs in the economy.
   (c) does not change the composition of employment in any industries.
   (d) is more important in determining labor market conditions than overall macroeconomic policy.

7. Which of the following is TRUE?
   (a) Manufacturing is more difficult to automate than services.
   (b) Manufacturing has faster rates of productivity growth than services.
   (c) It now takes more people to produce the manufactured products that we consume.
   (d) When incomes rise, we consume more services and manufactured goods, and the share of our total employment in each sector remains relatively constant.

8. What seems to be the primary culprit for the decline in wages of low-skill workers in advanced industrial economies?
   (a) Technological change
   (b) Government policy
   (c) Recession
   (d) Trade

9. In the HO model, comparative advantage is based
   (a) on differences in wages.
   (b) on differences in absolute advantage.
   (c) on having similar inputs.
   (d) on differences in factor endowments.

10. In the product cycle, consumption in high income countries would exceed production
    (a) in the early phase.
    (b) in the middle phase.
    (c) in the late phase.
    (d) never.

■ Answers to Vocabulary

1. factor abundance
2. factor scarcity
3. Heckscher-Ohlin (HO) trade theory
4. derived demand
5. Stolper-Samuelson theorem
6. magnification effect
7. specific factors model
8. product cycle
9. intra-firm trade
10. OLI theory

■ Answers to Chapter Review

1. They believed each country would have its own technology, climate, and resources and natural differences between nations would give rise to productivity differences.

2. Differences in the endowments of inputs or factors of production used to produce the products.

3. Nations differ in the level of specific factors of production they possess and products differ in the "recipe" or combinations of factors of production that they require.

4. A country's comparative advantage will be in the production of goods that use its relatively abundant factors of production.

5. In the simple Ricardian model, there was one input, labor, which was homogenous. It could be used to make either product and every worker was identical, so the trade off or opportunity cost was constant as workers were moved from one type of production to the other. In the HO Model, there are various types of inputs and workers may work with various combinations and amounts of inputs to produce various types of output. Workers may differ in their knowledge and abilities. This means that the production possibilities curve will no longer be a straight line and that opportunity costs will be increasing because resources are not perfectly adaptable from one type of production process to another.

6. Because opportunity costs are increasing, as production increases the costs increase. Eventually it will cease to be cheaper to produce the product in this nation due to rising costs.

7. The owners of capital will see an increase in demand for capital and an increase in their incomes. The owners of labor will see less demand for labor and a decrease in their incomes as they cannot be as easily absorbed in the capital intensive industry.

8. The change in output has a magnified effect on factors incomes, meaning a percentage change in the price of the output will cause a larger percentage change in the income of the factor of production used intensively in its production.

9. The input's flexibility in being able to move to alternate types of production.

10. In the short run, in Belgium land owners will see a decrease in their incomes and capital owners will see an increase. Workers will gain from lower olive prices but will see higher prices for beer. In Portugal, land owners' incomes will rise and capital owners' incomes will fall. Workers will gain from lower beer prices but will have higher olive prices.

11. It is difficult to measure factor endowments because the range of factors of production is so varied and there are no standardized measuring tools across nations, so it has been difficult to empirically assess the HO model. The Ricardian model is more easily tested and relative differences in labor productivities do seem to predict the trade patterns between pairs of nations.

12. Manufactured products go through a product cycle in which inputs change over time. The changes in the inputs needed to produce the product at various points in the cycle lead to changes in production location as the necessary comparative advantage shifts from high-income countries to low-income countries.

13. The early phase is characterized by experimentation in both the product and the manufacturing process used to produce it. Sophisticated marketing and consumer feedback mechanisms are some of the inputs needed that necessitate manufacturing being near a high-income market. Experimentation and improvement in design and manufacturing require scientific and engineering inputs and capital that is willing to risk failure and some periods of little or no profits.

14. The product becomes standardized in size, features, and the manufacturing process. Production begins to shift to countries with low labor costs as manufacturing routines are standardized, assembly-type operations.

15. While it is a more elaborate story about technological change, fundamentally product cycle theory is still about comparative advantage and opportunity costs. In the early stage, opportunity costs are lower in high-income countries because of their unique resource endowments. In the later stages, opportunity costs are lower in low-wage countries as the factors of production in the manufacturing process shift to being more labor intensive.

16. Firms invest abroad rather than exporting as the opportunity costs of producing in low-wage nations falls. They then import the now standardized product back to the home market where it was originally developed.

17. U.S. industries expected to gain from NAFTA include agriculture cereal or grain crops used for human or animal consumption and oilseeds. Advanced manufacturing was also expected to gain, including telecommunications, computing, aircraft, measuring and control devices, and chemicals. High-wage, skilled service industries such as banking, insurance, business services, and engineering were also expected to expand. U.S. industries expected to be hurt by NAFTA include the garment and apparel industry, leather goods, furniture, and building materials. In agriculture, labor intensive fruit and vegetable crops such as frozen vegetables, citrus, and avocados.

18. If the company has an asset that they need to control production in order to protect and needs to produce in a particular location to reduce transport or other costs or to have access to a specific market, it is more likely to invest abroad than to trade. The decision is complicated and relies on numerous factors brought together loosely under the variables ownership-location-internalization.

19. automatic data processing equipment, telecommunications equipment and parts for office machines or data processing machines

20. Highly educated and more skilled workers

■ Answers to Just the Facts

1. China; India
2. commercial aircraft; grain and grain products
3. constant; increasing
4. more units
5. an increase; rise
6. larger
7. Raymond Vernon
8. early
9. John Dunning
10. ownership
11. location
12. internalization
13. decreased
14. increased; younger; less schooling or fewer skills

15. productivity gains
16. more; less; technology

■ Answers to For Practice

1. (a) 1/2
    (b) 1/4
    (c) South Africa
    (d) Nigeria
    (e) mining
    (f) labor

2. (a) 1/4
    (b) 1/6
    (c) Brazil
    (d) Peru
    (e) Brazil
    (f) Labor

■ Answers to Review Quiz

1. D
2. D
3. C
4. C
5. C
6. A
7. B
8. A
9. D
10. C

Chapter 5
Beyond Comparative Advantage

■ Vocabulary

For each numbered description, write in the correct term from the list provided.

agglomeration
external economies of scale
externality
Grubel-Lloyd index
industrial policy
interindustry trade
internal economies of scale
intraindusty trade
market failure
monopolistic competition
oligopoly
private return
product differentiation
rent seeking
social return
strategic trade policy
value added

1. The international trade of products within the same industry _____

2. The international trade of products between two different industries _____

3. A statistic that measures the amount of intraindustry trade _____

4. As a firm expands output, average production costs fall _____

5. Average production costs fall for an individual firm as its industry expands output _____

6. A market structure characterized by a relatively small number of firms who are aware of and responsive to one another _____

7. A market structure characterized by a relatively large number of firms that make products that are not perfect substitutes _____

8. Each firm produces output that is slightly different, giving it a unique advantage _____

9. Regional concentration of firms in the same industry _____

10. Government policies designed to create new industries or to support existing industries _____

11. When the private market economy fails to deliver the optimal quantity of goods and services _____

12. The costs and benefits of an economic activity that are experienced by the immediate parties to the transaction (usually the consumers and the producers of the product) _____

13. The costs and benefits of an economic activity to the overall society or market
_____

14. A market failure caused by the externalization of some of the costs or benefits of an economic activity, separating the private returns from the social returns _____

15. The selective use of trade barriers and industry subsidies to capture foreign firm profit in a situation where an industry has economies of scale and firms have market power _____

16. The difference between the cost of materials and the value of the output _____

17. Any activity by firms, individuals, or special interests that is designed to alter the distribution of income in their favor without adding to the amount of total income in the economy
_____

■ Chapter Review

Answer the questions in the space provided below each.

1. Describe the difference between intraindustry trade and interindustry trade.

2. What are internal economies of scale, and why are they an important feature of intraindustry trade?

3. Describe the gains from intraindustry trade.

4. Use U.S.-Canada merchandise trade to give examples of intraindustry trade and interindustry trade.

5. Describe how an agglomeration can lead to external economies of scale.

6. How might an agglomeration misallocate resources?

7. What are some of the reasons why social returns may be different from private returns?

8. What are the two essential ingredients for strategic trade policy?

9. What are the potential problems with implementing strategic trade policy?

10. What are the tools available to governments for industrial policy?

11. What are some of the potential problems with industrial policies?

12. What are the two periods in U.S. history that featured intense debate over industrial policy, and who was the United State's perceived rival at that time?

■ Just the Facts

1. A (large, small) share of international trade is not based on comparative advantage.

2. In world trade, countries (never, rarely, often) import the same products they export.

3. _____ and the United States have the largest trade relationship in the world, and much of that trade is within the _____ industry.

4. If countries have different factor endowments and productivities, their trade is likely to be (intraindustry, interindustry).

5. Intraindustry trade is measured for each industry with a statistic called the _____.

6. Probably more than _____ percent of total world trade is intraindustry.

7. Estimates suggest that between _____ and _____ of U.S. trade is intraindustry.

8. Trading Bass beer for Budweiser beer is an example of (intraindustry, interindustry) trade.

9. In 1965, the United States and Canada implemented a free-trade policy that covered _____.

10. _____ is an example of an agglomeration associated with the high-technology industry.

11. If the social returns are less than the private returns, a free market economy will produce (less, more) than the optimal amount of a product.

12. _____, _____, and _____ are three industries with a long history of support in the United States through subsidies.

■ For Practice

Calculate the Grubel-Lloyd index for the industries given below. The data are in millions of U.S. dollars and come from the U.S. Department of Commerce Bureau of Economic Analysis from the 2003 Balance of Payments.

Industry	Exports	Imports	GL Index
Airplanes	9,327	4,681	
Alcoholic beverages, distilled	187	1,360	
Chemicals, fertilizers	905	936	
Clothing	2,170	25,984	
Coffee	1	685	
Electrical machinery	28,005	32,792	
Footware	210	6,538	
Metal working machinery	1,627	2,144	
Oils/fats, vegetable	544	531	
Power generating machinery	12,838	13,629	
Vehicles	26,139	70,824	

■ Review Quiz

Check your mastery of the chapter by selecting the letter that gives the correct answer to each question.

1. Which of the following is true?
   (a) Trade models built exclusively on the idea of comparative advantage are excellent predictors of a country's trade patterns.
   (b) If we accurately measure comparative advantage, we will be able to predict import and export patterns.
   (c) The idea of comparative advantage is the foundation of our understanding of the gains from trade and the potential income distribution effects of trade.
   (d) It is relatively easy to measure a country's comparative advantage.

2. Which of the following is false?
   (a) There are many products a country might export that use the same comparative advantage.
   (b) Only a small share of international trade is not based on comparative advantage.
   (c) Given products that require the same comparative advantage, there is no way to predict in advance which ones might dominate in world markets.
   (d) It is exceedingly difficult to measure comparative advantage.

3. Which of the following is correct?
   (a) If the Grubel-Lloyd index equals one, all of the industry's trade is intraindustry.
   (b) If the Grubel-Lloyd index equals one, all of the industry's trade is interindustry.
   (c) If the Grubel-Lloyd index equals zero, all of the industry's trade is intraindustry.
   (d) If the Grubel-Lloyd index equals zero, the index cannot give us any information about the industry's trade pattern.

4. Which of the following is false?
   (a) Intraindustry trade is greater in high technology industries where the rapid generation of new products leads to greater product differentiation.
   (b) An important share of world trade consists of countries exporting the same thing they import.
   (c) The broader the definition of an industry, the more trade appears to be intraindustry.
   (d) Less than 20 percent of U.S. trade appears to be intraindustry.

5. Intraindustry trade tends to be greater
   (a) as a nation's income rises.
   (b) in industries with little product differentiation.
   (c) in countries with high trade barriers.
   (d) in industries that are not technologically innovative or generating new products rapidly.

6. The price of an exported product,
   (a) rises for domestic consumers with intraindustry trade.
   (b) falls for domestic consumers with interindustry trade.
   (c) falls for domestic consumers with intraindustry trade.
   (d) may rise or fall in the case of interindustry trade.

7. The 1965 auto trade agreement between the United States and Canada,
   (a) led Canadian automakers to produce a greater number of models.
   (b) significantly increased Canadian auto productivity.
   (c) led to less choice for Canadian consumers of autos as some Canadian firms failed.
   (d) was unsuccessful in helping Canadian automakers gain from potential economies of scale.

8. The largest bilateral trade relationship in the world exists between
   (a) the United States and Canada.
   (b) the United States and Japan.
   (c) the United States and Mexico.
   (d) China and Japan.

9. Which of the following is true?
   (a) Geography and distance have been completely conquered by recent advances in telecommunications.
   (b) Start up firms do not seem willing to pay higher costs to locate in regions that are hubs for their industry.
   (c) For some types of firms there seems to be large financial benefits to geographical clustering.
   (d) In the modern era of communication technology, high-tech start ups have not followed the pattern of clustering observed in other industries.

10. Which of the following is false? When a firm joins a regional industrial cluster, it
    (a) obtains advantages for itself in terms of lower costs through external economies of scale.
    (b) enhances the competitiveness of the other firms in the cluster.
    (c) strengthens the country's export performance.
    (d) reduces its costs only if it is able to become a larger firm.

11. Comparative advantage
    (a) is immutable; it cannot be changed.
    (b) can change, but cannot be affected by government policy.
    (c) can change as a result of government policies and spending on programs such as education and infrastructure development over time.
    (d) is easily changed by government policies targeting the development of specific new industries.

12. If the private returns to an activity are less than the social returns, the free market will
    (a) allocate too few resources to the activity for economic efficiency.
    (b) allocate too many resources to the activity for economic efficiency.
    (c) allocate the efficient amount of resources to the activity.
    (d) may overallocate or underallocate resources depending on the situation.

13. All of the following are potential problems with implementing strategic trade policy, except
    (a) WTO rules make it difficult for nations to offer direct subsidies to domestic firms.
    (b) using subsidies to target a key industry might spark a trade war.
    (c) industry costs and profits are easy for governments to calculate and anticipate.
    (d) foreign governments might offer counter subsidies to their domestic firms.

■ Answers to Vocabulary

1. intraindusty trade
2. interindustry trade
3. Grubel-Lloyd index
4. internal economies of scale
5. external economies of scale
6. oligopoly
7. monopolistic competition
8. product differentiation
9. agglomeration
10. industrial policy
11. market failure
12. private return
13. social return
14. externality
15. strategic trade policy
16. value added
17. rent seeking

Answers to Chapter Review

1. Interindustry trade is the type of trade presented in Chapters 3 and 4, where nations trade products that are completely different and require different types of factors of production or different productivities to produce. Intraindustry trade is where products are traded for similar products in the same industry. These products require the same types of resources and similar factor productivities to produce.

2. When a firm's average costs fall as output increases over a relatively large range of output, internal economies of scale exist. This makes firms want to enter export markets because as output expands, costs fall. For any given number of firms, average costs are lower in a larger market.

3. Lower costs and competition lead to lower prices for consumers for both the imported and exported product. The fact that both exports and imports are at lower prices increases real income. Firms produce at a higher level of efficiency given the increase in market size. Because of the expansion in size of the industry, intraindustry trade is generally less threatening to jobs and firms than interindustry trade. Trade is likely to expand the number of domestic firms and output. Consumers have more choices.

4. Trade in autos and auto parts dominates the major exports and imports of the United States and Canada, which is an example of intraindustry trade. The United States also imports from Canada natural gas and crude oil, which are both based on Canada's natural resource endowments and would be an example of interindustry, comparative advantage based trade.

5. Close physical proximity enhances knowledge spillovers that keep all firms abreast of the latest technology and newest developments. Information can be exchanged through both formal and informal networks, and this is particularly important in frontier industries undergoing rapid technological change. Labor markets deepen for highly specialized skills, which reduces search costs and gives firms a choice of workers with the best skills. Dense networks of highly specialized input suppliers can also develop. All of these function to enhance production and to reduce costs.

6. Agglomerations become self-reinforcing. Small initial differences in costs lead to feedback mechanisms that create large differences in costs based on production location. Hypothetically, a region could get an early advantage, form an agglomeration, and the cost advantages of the agglomeration may prevent the development of the industry in another location that could have been more efficient. Production is thus concentrated with the less efficient producer because the more efficient producer never has the chance to get off the ground.

7. Knowledge spillovers, spillovers from research and development of new products and technology, and capital market imperfections are all potential reasons why social returns and private returns might not be equal.

8. Industry must have economies of scale and firms must have market power that enables them to earn above normal profits.

9. Subsidies are against WTO rules, foreign governments might offer counter subsidies or retaliate with a trade war, and it is difficult for the government to have detailed information about costs and likely profits for industries.

10. Within WTO rules, governments can subsidize pre-competitive activities such as research. They can provide information about foreign markets, help negotiate contracts, lobby foreign governments to purchase products and adopt home-country standards, and tie foreign aid to purchases of home-country products. Some governments sell foreign exchange to targeted firms at below-market rates or offer loans at below-market interest rates. They can provide special tax treatment or use their own purchases to help specific industries. They can encourage firms to work together by funding research or relaxing anti-trade laws. Governments may directly own and operate firms.

11. Governments lack sufficient information to provide the right resources to the right industries and to correctly anticipate foreign firms' responses. Positive externalities from new innovations are usually a surprise to everyone involved and are difficult to correctly anticipate. Industrial policy encourages rent seeking. The spending of resources on rent seeking reduces efficiency. It is impossible to contain the external benefits of successful research and development within the national borders once innovation does occur.

12. In the 1790s the United States feared domination by Great Britain. In the 1970s and '80s, Japanese technological and manufacturing superiority was feared.

■ Answers to Just the Facts

1. large
2. often
3. Canada; auto
4. interindustry
5. Grubel-Lloyd (GL) index
6. 40
7. 1/3; 2/3
8. intraindustry
9. autos and auto parts
10. Silicon Valley
11. more
12. transportation infrastructure; agriculture; defense

■ Answer to For Practice

airplanes, 0.67; distilled alcoholic beverages, 0.24; chemicals for fertilizers, 0.98; clothing, 0.15; coffee, 0; electrical machinery, 0.92; footware, 0.06; metal working machinery, 0.86; vegetable oils/fats, 0.99; power generating machinery, 0.97; vehicles, 0.54.

■ Answers to Review Quiz

1. C
2. B
3. A
4. D
5. A
6. C
7. B
8. A

9. C
10. D
11. C
12. A
13. C

Chapter 6
The Theory of Tariffs and Quotas

■ Vocabulary

For each numbered description, write in the correct term from the list provided.

consumer surplus
deadweight loss
effective rate of protection
efficiency loss
large country case
nominal rate of protection

nontariff barrier (NTB)
nontransparent
producer surplus
quota
quota rent

rent seeking
tariff
transparent
value added
voluntary export restraint (VER)

1. Obvious or easily observable _____

2. Hidden or hard to observe or gather information about _____

3. Tax on internationally traded products _____

4. Quantitative limit on the volume of internationally traded products _____

5. The excess value consumers receive, above and beyond the prices they pay, for the products they purchase, reflected on a graph as the gap between the demand curve and the market price
_____

6. Any activity by firms, individuals, or special interests that is designed to alter the distribution of income in their favor without adding to the amount of total income in the economy
_____

7. A destruction of value that is not compensated by a gain somewhere else _____

8. A loss caused when domestic firms expand output at higher costs than the world price because of protection _____

9. In theory, because of its size, a country may have market power and might be able to improve its national welfare with a tariff as long as its trading partners don't retaliate _____

10. The tariff that is levied on a given product _____

11. The tariff that is levied on a product taking into account any tariffs on intermediate inputs
    _____

12. The price of a good minus the costs of the intermediate goods used to produce it
    _____

13. An exporting country agrees to limit its exports for some period of time, usually after a series of negotiations where the exporter may be threatened with more severe restrictions
    _____

14. Greater profits for foreign firms as a result of quantitative restrictions on imports rather than tariffs
    _____

15. Quotas and other nontariff measures that restrict trade _____

16. The amount firms receive above and beyond what they would be willing to produce the product for, reflected on a graph as the gap between the market price and the supply curve
    _____

■ Chapter Review

Answer the questions in the space provided below each.

1. What is the difference between a tariff and a quota?

2. What effect do tariffs and quotas have on consumers?

3. Who benefits from tariffs and who is harmed? Use the concepts of consumer surplus and producer surplus to describe the gains and losses.

4. What are some other potential costs of tariffs?

5. How might large countries gain from imposing a tariff? What role does market power play?

6. Why are effective rates more important than nominal rates of protection?

7. How are negative rates of protection possible?

8. What is the main difference between tariffs and quotas?

9. What are the three major types of quotas?

10. Before they were limited by the Uruguay Round, voluntary export restraints were popular. Why?

11. Over time, how do quotas compare with tariffs?

12. Describe other nontariff barriers to trade.

13. What were some of the results of U.S. voluntary export restraints on Japanese autos in the 1980s?

■ Just the Facts

1. In general, tariffs in the industrial world today are (high, low).

2. Trade barriers in _____, _____, and _____ are relatively high.

3. If the effective rate of protection is (less than, greater than, equal to) the nominal rate of protection, there must be tariffs on intermediate products.

4. Both tariffs and quotas lead to (an increase, a decrease, no change) in imports, (an increase, a decrease, no change) in domestic consumption, and (an increase, a decrease, no change) in domestic production.

5. High-income countries are likely to have (higher, lower, similar) tariffs than low-income countries.

6. Average tariffs fell by about _____ percent between 1986 and 2001.

7. Tariff revenue is an important source of operating revenue for many governments of (high-income, middle-income, low-income) countries.

8. The total cost to U.S. consumers of the VER agreement for autos in the early 1980s is estimated to be _____ billion. Of this, _____ was transferred to domestic producers from domestic consumers.

9. An estimated _____ jobs were saved by the VERs in the U.S. auto industry at a cost of _____ per job saved.

10. The European Community banned U.S. _____ from the EC market in 1988 over health concerns about growth hormones.

11. Quotas lead to (smaller, larger, similar) deadweight losses as tariffs.

12. (Quotas, licensing agreements, voluntary export restraints) are the most transparent limitation on the volume of imports.

For Practice

1. Use the graph below to answer questions (a)–(j). Assume the world price is $1.50 per unit and the government puts a $0.50 per unit tariff on the product.

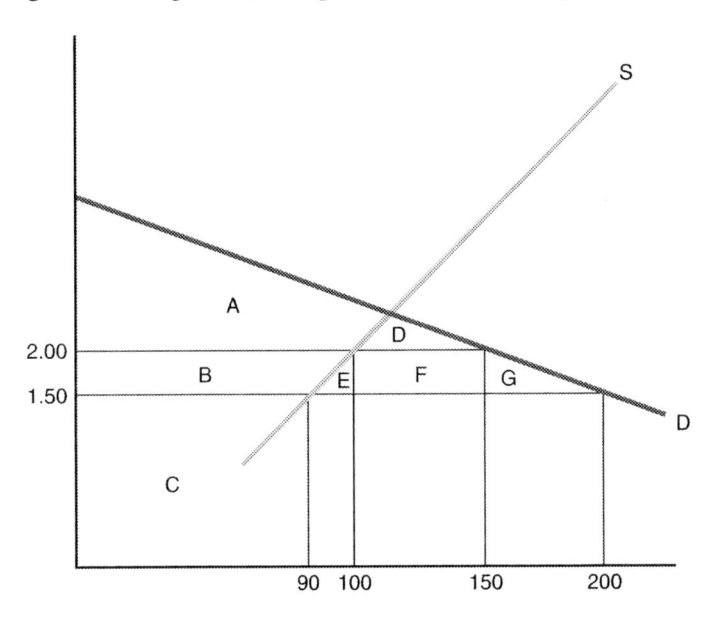

    (a) Which letter(s) correspond to the area(s) that make up consumer surplus under free trade?
    (b) Which letter(s) correspond to the area(s) that make up producer surplus under free trade?
    (c) Which letter(s) correspond to the area(s) that represents the loss in consumer surplus due to the tariff?
    (d) Which letter(s) correspond to the area(s) that represents the increase in producer surplus due to the tariff?
    (e) Which letter(s) correspond to the government revenue collected from the tariff?
    (f) Which letter(s) correspond to the national loss from the tarriff?
    (g) Which letter(s) correspond to the efficiency loss from the tariff?
    (h) Which letter(s) correspond to the deadweight loss from the tariff?
    (i) How much does the tariff reduce imports?
    (j) How much does the tariff increase domestic production?

2. Calculate missing values for the domestic value added and the effective rate of protection in the table below.

	No Tariff	30 Percent on Final Product	30 Percent Tariff Plus 40 Percent Tariff on Imported Inputs
Price of a cellular phone	100	130	130
Value of foreign inputs	50	50	70
Domestic value added	50		
Effective rate of protection	0		

Review Quiz

Check your mastery of the chapter by selecting the letter that gives the correct answer to each question.

1. Tariffs lead to all of the following except:
   (a) higher prices for domestic consumers.
   (b) an increase in government revenue.
   (c) higher prices for domestic firms.
   (d) higher prices for foreign producers of the product.

2. Which of the following is true?
   (a) Tariffs are more transparent than nontariff barriers to trade.
   (b) Quotas lead to smaller deadweight losses than tariffs.
   (c) Tariffs lead to higher prices in the short run than do quotas.
   (d) Imports are easier to adjust under quotas than under tariffs if there is a change in domestic demand.

3. If a tariff is reduced,
   (a) domestic consumer surplus increases.
   (b) domestic producer surplus increases.
   (c) government revenue increases.
   (d) deadweight losses increase.

4. In the long run,
   (a) tariffs allow domestic firms to gain additional producer surplus from any future increases in demand for the product
   (b) quotas are quite easy to eliminate because firms won't seek to keep the protection once they have temporarily acquired it
   (c) both tariffs and quotas reduce domestic firms' incentives to innovate and to be more efficient
   (d) quotas generate more government revenue than tariffs

5. If a product sells for $250 and the value of imported parts is $150, the domestic value added is:
   (a) $50
   (b) $100
   (c) $150
   (d) $250

6. Tariffs on final goods and services raise the price of the product. With no tariffs on inputs and no change in any other factor, this means that domestic value added _____ when the tariff is imposed.
   (a) will fall
   (b) will stay the same
   (c) will rise
   (d) may rise or fall

7. Suppose the world price of coffee makers is $20.00 and that the value of imported intermediate goods used to produce coffee makers in the United States is $12.00. If the U.S. government imposes a 10 percent tariff on coffee makers, what is the effective rate of protection?
   (a) 5 percent
   (b) 10 percent
   (c) 20 percent
   (d) 25 percent

8. Suppose the world price of coffee makers is $20.00 and that the value of imported intermediate goods used to produce coffee makers in the United States is $12.00. If the U.S. government imposes a 10 percent tariff on coffee makers and an additional 50 percent tariff on the imported intermediate goods used to produce coffee makers, what is the effective rate of protection?
   (a) −75 percent
   (b) −50 percent
   (c) −25 percent
   (d) 10 percent

Use the graph below to answer questions 9–12. Assume the world price is $5.00.

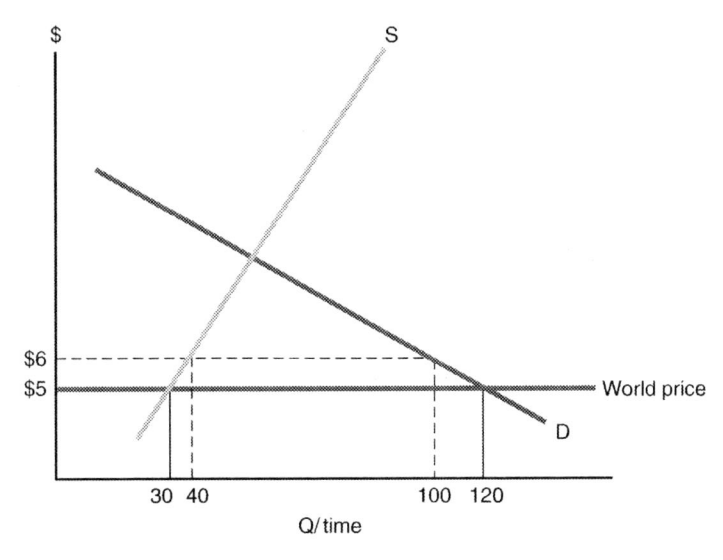

9. If the government imposes a tariff of $1.00 per unit, imports will be reduced _____ units.
   (a) 10
   (b) 20
   (c) 30
   (d) 60

10. If the government imposes a tariff of $1.00 per unit, domestic production will increase _____ units.
   (a) 10
   (b) 30
   (c) 40
   (d) 100

11. If the government imposes a tariff of $1.00 per unit, it will collect _____ in revenue from the tariff.
    (a) $40
    (b) $60
    (c) $100
    (d) $600

12. Suppose the government wanted to use a quota instead of a tariff to achieve the same amount of protection for domestic firms as shown above. Which of the following is false?
    (a) The government would likely forgo revenue it is currently earning under the tariff.
    (b) Foreign firms would receive higher prices than they are under the tariff.
    (c) The deadweight losses would be smaller than they are with the tariff.
    (d) The quota would be set at 60 units to achieve the same protection for firms as the $1 per unit tariff.

■ Answers to Vocabulary

1. transparent
2. nontransparent
3. tariff
4. quota
5. consumer surplus
6. rent seeking
7. deadweight loss
8. efficiency loss
9. large country case
10. nominal rate of protection
11. effective rate of protection
12. value added
13. voluntary export restraint (VER)
14. quota rent
15. nontariff barrier (NTB)
16. producer surplus

■ Answers to Chapter Review

1. Tariffs are a tax placed on internationally traded products, while quotas are a restriction on the volume of goods allowed to be traded.

2. Because they raise the product's price, they cause some consumers to switch to domestically produced goods and services and others to stop buying the product all together. They reduce both consumer surplus and imports.

3. Domestic firms benefit from tariffs. They sell more units and producer surplus increases. The domestic government is able to collect revenue from tariffs, although how important this revenue is to the overall government depends on the other tax systems in place. Consumers lose. Consumer surplus decreases more than the combined increase in producer surplus and government revenue, leading to national losses from the tariff.

4. Retaliation by foreign governments can hurt the export markets of other industries. Tariffs isolate domestic firms from foreign competition and reduce the incentive to innovate new products, to become more efficient, or to upgrade the existing product. Firms often devote resources to seeking protection or to keeping protection in place, which is known as rent seeking.

5. As a large purchaser of the imported product, the domestic country may be able to influence the price foreign firms charge through the use of a tariff. The fact that the large country is buying less after the tariff makes the foreign firms discount the price, effectively decreasing the world price. The size of the deadweight losses are reduced because imports do not fall as much and domestic production does not grow as much given the discounted price. The government collects extra revenue from the foreign firms, which may offset the deadweight losses.

6. Effective rates of protection take into account both the value added by domestic firms to the final product and any tariffs on intermediate products. It gives a much clearer picture of the overall amount of protection any given product receives.

7. If intermediate inputs face tariffs, effective rates of protection can be negative. Tariffs are influenced by domestic lobbyists, strategic interests, and other pressures, and are not planned in a coherent, systematic fashion. Newer tariffs may undo the effects of older tariffs.

8. Quotas generally do not create any government revenue and therefore have larger national losses from protection.

9. Formal quotas are an outright limitation on the quantity of imports. Import licensing requirements are less transparent. Voluntary export restraints or voluntary restraint agreements have the exporting country "voluntarily" limit its own exports in exchange for no other formal trade barriers.

10. They did not require legislative action so they were quick to enact. Because they are "negotiated," they do not seem as protectionist as other forms of trade barriers. They also represented a way around prior agreements to restrict tariffs, but this loophole was closed in the Uruguay Round.

11. With tariffs, as many units can be imported as desired as long as the tariff is paid, so increases in domestic demand would result in more imports, and in the small country case, no change in price. With quotas, increases in domestic demand have to be met by the domestic market since the volume of imports is set by the quota. Domestic firms will see an increase in producer surplus as a result of the higher prices caused by the increase in domestic demand.

12. Domestic governments can, in their own purchasing, discriminate against foreign suppliers. In some countries, whole industries are owned by the government, which effectively shuts off foreign competition. Esoteric or unclear safety standards, special product certification, and excessive government bureaucracy can be barriers. Local content requirements may be used.

13. Higher prices for both domestic and foreign cars, lost consumer surplus, some jobs saved, Japanese firms entered higher-end portion of U.S. auto market and located some manufacturing in the United States.

■ Answers to Just the Facts

1. low
2. agriculture, textiles and apparel
3. less than
4. a decrease, a decrease, an increase
5. lower
6. 50
7. low-income
8. $5.8 billion, $2.6 billion
9. 55,000, $105,000
10. livestock (beef and pork)
11. larger
12. quotas

■ Answers to For Practice

1. (a) A, B, D, E, F, G
   (b) C
   (c) B, E, F, G
   (d) B
   (e) F
   (f) E, G
   (g) E
   (h) G
   (i) 60 units
   (j) 10 units

2. with 30 percent tariff on final product only, the value added is 80 and the effective rate of protection is 60 percent. With the tariff on both the final goods and the intermediate goods, the value added is 60 and the effective rate of protection is 20 percent.

■ Answers to Review Quiz

1. D
2. A
3. A
4. C
5. B

6. C
7. D
8. B
9. C
10. A
11. B
12.

Chapter 7
Commercial Policy

■ Vocabulary

For each numbered description, write in the correct term from the list provided.

antidumping duty	escape clause relief	infant industry
countervailing duty	externality	Section 301 and Super 301
dumping	fair value	subsidy

1. An argument for protection mainly associated with developing nations that protect their industries from competition with more mature firms in industrialized countries _____

2. Costs or benefits of a transaction borne by someone other than the immediate producer or consumer _____

3. A tariff granted to an industry that has been hurt by foreign country subsidies of its national firms, the goal being to raise the price of the foreign good high enough to offset any advantage from the subsidy _____

4. Could be a direct loan or transfer from the government to a firm, preferential tax treatment, the government supplying goods and services other than infrastructure, or providing firms with income or price supports _____

5. Tariff levied on an import that is selling at a price below the product's fair value _____

6. Selling a product in a foreign market at a price below what is charged in the home market _____

7. Determining this is difficult and subjective _____

8. A part of U.S. and GATT trade rules that allows a temporary tariff to be imposed to protect an industry from a sudden surge in imports so the industry has time to adjust _____

9. U.S. trade law that requires action against nations that engage in unfair trade practices _____

■ Chapter Review

Answer the questions in the space provided below each.

1. Describe the overall level of trade barriers for the United States, Japan and the European Union and address any sectors that are an exception to this pattern.

2. If tariffs are low, why should we care about them?

3. What conclusions does your text reach about protection of agriculture, textiles and clothing in the United States, Japan and the European Union?

4. Why was the Uruguay Round significant?

5. What are the four arguments nations use to justify protecting their industries?

6. What is the primary failure of the labor argument? What is a secondary failure?

7. What two beliefs underline the infant industry argument?

8. For protection to work in the infant industry case, what else must happen?

9. What is the national security argument? What problems does this argument pose for economic analysis?

10. On what does the outcome of retaliation depend?

11. How can closing a domestic market create advantages for domestic firms that engage in foreign competition elsewhere?

12. When are economic sanctions most effective?

13. What are the five ways protection in the United States may be achieved?

14. How do the legal procedures for protection get initiated?

15. Which part of government does the investigation in the case of subsidies and dumping?

16. Which part of government determines if harm has been caused by subsidies and dumping and if protection is warranted from these or from a sudden surge in imports?

17. In the Doha Development Agenda, which three agricultural issues are being discussed?

■ Just the Facts

1. In 2001, average nominal tariff rates were _____ in the United States, _____ in Japan, and _____ in the European Union.

2. The European Union, the United States, and Japan all provide _____ to some of their agricultural producers.

3. The overall level of tariffs and quotas in the United States and Japan is (high, low, average) for industrialized nations.

4. In the United States after the Uruguay round, World Bank data shows that while average tariffs fell 40 percent, tariffs on agricultural goods fell _____ percent, and clothing and textile tariffs fell _____ percent each.

5. In addition to tariffs, the U.S., E.U., and Japanese governments have significant _____ for agriculture, clothing and textiles.

6. Quota rents are earned by (domestic producers, domestic government, foreign producers) and (reduce, increase, do not affect) national welfare.

7. In the European Union and Japan, the largest national losses from protection occur in (agriculture, textiles, clothing).

8. In the United States, the largest national losses from protection occur in (agriculture, textiles, clothing).

9. Japan is one of the world's largest (exporters, importers) of agricultural products and the United States is one of the world's largest (exporters, importers) of clothing.

10. For Japan in agriculture and for the U.S. in clothing, protection leads to large national losses in the form of _____ .

11. In each of the sectors and in each of the countries studied, the cost per job saved of protection exceeded _____ per year.

12. In Japan and the United States, jobs in (agriculture, textiles, clothing) were the most expensive to save.

13. In the European Union, jobs in (agriculture, textiles, clothing) were the most expensive to save.

14. The costs of tariffs and quotas are (spread out, concentrated), while the benefits are (spread out, concentrated).

15. Economic sanctions alone may be ineffective in achieving difficult goals. In that case, countries may use _____ to back up the sanctions and make the desired change.

16. The use of (countervailing duties, antidumping duties, escape clause relief, Section 301) is growing and has become a significant source of trade tension.

■ Review Quiz

Check your mastery of the chapter by selecting the letter that gives the correct answer to each question.

1. Which of the following is false?
    (a) Very few countries apply tariffs uniformly across all industries.
    (b) Many countries provide generous subsidies to some of their agricultural producers.
    (c) Even low tariffs have a high ratio of costs to benefits.
    (d) Tariffs and quotas are an efficient way of protecting jobs.

2. Which of the following is true?
    (a) In nearly all leading industrialized countries, agriculture, textiles, and clothing are relatively free from trade barriers.
    (b) While subsidies are not explicitly trade barriers, they have the same import-reducing effect as tariffs and quotas.
    (c) The overall level of tariffs and quotas in the United States and Japan is relatively high for industrialized nations.
    (d) The benefits of tariffs and quotas for job creation outweigh the costs of protection.

3. Agriculture, clothing, and textile trade barriers have been subjects of intense international debate because
    (a) high-income countries would likely be successful in these industries without protection.
    (b) high-income countries are hurting other powerful, high-income countries with this protection.
    (c) developing countries could be major consumers of these products if they weren't so highly protected.
    (d) developing countries have significant comparative advantages in these production lines.

4. Commercial policy
    (a) is very effective at preserving jobs.
    (b) is grossly inefficient at preserving jobs.
    (c) is the only tool available to preserve jobs.
    (d) never has unintended consequences.

5. When tariffs are low,
    (a) the costs per job saved are also low.
    (b) they are a good tool for job preservation.
    (c) the costs per job saved tend to be high.
    (d) they do not cause much losses to national welfare.

6. The costs of tariffs and quotas are
   (a) never known.
   (b) low.
   (c) concentrated on a few major purchasers.
   (d) spread out over a large number of buyers.

7. The economist Mancur Olson found
   (a) there was symmetry in the incentives to support and to oppose protectionist policies.
   (b) the benefits of protection were spread out over a number of firms and industries.
   (c) the costs of protection were concentrated on a few key consumers.
   (d) there was asymmetry in the incentives to support and to oppose protectionist policies.

8. Major breakthroughs accomplished by the Uruguay round of trade negotiations include all of the following except
   (a) the inclusion of subsidies in an agreement for the first time.
   (b) the inclusion of agriculture and textiles for the first time.
   (c) agreements on trade in services.
   (d) agreements on intellectual property rights protection.

9. Which tool of U.S. trade policy is used the least?
   (a) Countervailing duties
   (b) Section 301
   (c) Antidumping duties
   (d) Escape clause relief

10. Countervailing duties are used when
    (a) there is a sudden surge of imports in the short run and temporary protection is needed.
    (b) dumping has occurred.
    (c) foreign trade practices are judged to be unfair to U.S. interests.
    (d) foreign firms are receiving subsidies.

11. Direct subsidies in agriculture are viewed as harmful because
    (a) they increase imports.
    (b) they raise the incomes of farm families.
    (c) they lead to overproduction.
    (d) they discourage dumping.

12. The biggest subsidizer of agriculture is
    (a) the European Union.
    (b) Japan.
    (c) the United States.
    (d) Brazil.

■ Answers to Vocabulary

1. infant industry
2. externality
3. countervailing duty
4. subsidy
5. antidumping duty
6. dumping
7. fair value
8. escape clause relief
9. Section 301 and Super 301

■ Answers to Chapter Review

1. In general, tariffs have fallen significantly and for high-income, industrialized countries, the average level of tariffs for industrial products is low. But some products and some industries enjoy significantly higher levels of protection. Agriculture, clothing and textiles remain heavily protected in all three areas.

2. Even low tariffs have a high ratio of costs to benefits and are not generally the most efficient way for nations to achieve employment and growth.

3. Protection imposes large national losses, partially in the form of quota rents to foreign producers since the countries often remain major importers of the product after protection. At a cost per job saved of more than $100,000, protection is grossly inefficient as a tool for job preservation. Keeping alive old industries where the nation has lost its comparative advantage not only creates national losses, it may impose costs on the developing nations the high-income countries are often trying to assist through other aid programs.

4. For the first time, agriculture and textiles were included and agreements were reached on services, intellectual property protection and foreign investment. Institutional reform created a superstructure called the World Trade Organization to administer all the agreements, to oversee a new dispute resolution process and trade policy reviews.

5. The labor argument, the infant industry argument, the national security argument, and the retaliation argument.

6. It fails to consider productivity differences. If preserving jobs is something worth devoting resources, other policies (such as fiscal, monetary, and labor market ones) are much more efficient at job creation and preservation than are trade barriers.

7. First is that market forces will not support the development of a particular industry given the already established foreign competition or the level of risk. Second is that the industry in question has external benefits that make it more valuable to the national economy than just its own wages and profits. These externalities are usually technological or in the form of a linkage to other existing industries.

8. The industry must experience falling average costs as output expands and the protection must be for a limited time period.

9. For military or defense reasons or to protect broad national cultural identity, certain products can either not be traded or can be traded in only a limited fashion. Security and cultural identity are non-economic values so it is harder to use the tools of economic analysis to come up with definitive answers.

10. It depends on political processes that determine how nations respond to pressure, their willingness to negotiate, and the outcome of the negotiation. Retaliation can provide an incentive for negotiation or it can provoke a trade war.

11. If market size is important, the ability to sell to a larger market (protected home + foreign), may give the domestic firms an advantage. If there are economies of scale, larger markets mean lower per unit costs that may force foreign rivals out of business, reducing choices, technologies, skills, and expertise.

12. The target country is small, economically weak, and politically unstable. The target country is a friendly ally. Sanctions are imposed quickly and decisively. The costs to the sending country are small. The goal is a relatively small change.

13. Direct action from the President, countervailing duties, antidumping duties, escape clause relief, Section 301 retaliations

14. A firm, an industry trade association, or a government agency may petition the federal government to initiate an investigation.

15. The International Trade Administration in the Department of Commerce

16. The United States International Trade Commission

17. Increasing market access through reducing tariffs and quotas, export subsidies given by countries to encourage farm exports, and production subsidies granted directly to farmers

■ Answers to Just the Facts

1. 4 percent; 5.1 percent; 3.9 percent
2. subsidies
3. average
4. 12; 14
5. nontariff barriers
6. foreign producers; reduce
7. agriculture
8. clothing
9. importers; importers
10. quota rents
11. $100,000

12. agriculture
13. textiles
14. spread out; concentrated
15. military force
16. antidumping duties

■ Answers to Review Quiz

1. D
2. B
3. D
4. B
5. C
6. D
7. D
8. A
9. B
10. D
11. C
12. A

Chapter 8
International Trade and Labor and Environmental Standards

■ Vocabulary

For each numbered description, write in the correct term from the list provided.

core labor standards
harmonization of standards
informal economy
International Labor Organization (ILO)
low-income country
lower-middle income country
upper-middle income country
high-income country
mutual recognition of standards
pollution haven
race to the bottom
separate standards
transboundary environmental problem
non-transboundary environmental problem

1. A nation with per capita income less than $736 in 2002 _____

2. A nation with per capita income between $736 and $2935 in 2002 _____

3. A nation with per capita income between $2,936 and $9075 in 2002 _____

4. A nation with per capita income greater than or equal to $9076 in 2002 _____

5. Setting the lowest possible level of standards _____

6. Two or more countries share a common set of standards in areas of concern, such as product safety and labor and environmental protection _____

7. Countries keep their own product and process standards but accept the standards of others as equally valid and sufficient _____

8. Countries keep their own product and process standards and refuse to recognize the standards of any other nation _____

9. A part of the economy that is untaxed, unregulated, and uninspected _____

10. Started in 1919 and seeks the promotion of social justice and internationally recognized human and labor rights _____

11. Eight standards the ILO believes all nations should respect _____

12. Environmental issues or standards of one country that affect only that country _____

13. Environmental issues or standards of one country that affect other countries _____

14. Country that competes by offering firms a reduced set of environmental compliance _____

■ Chapter Review

Answer the questions in the space provided below each.

1. What does your text identify as two obstacles of increased international economic integration?

2. Give examples of conflicts over standards and explain why they occur.

3. What are the options available in terms of setting standards for nations seeking to expand their commercial ties? Describe each.

4. Why might harmonization of standards be useful in the case of technology? When might it be harmful?

5. In general, which environmental indicators get worse as income rises and which get better?

6. How does national income correlate with child mortality and child labor?

7. What five labor standards does the International Labor Organization propose?

8. For low-income countries, why is it difficult to reduce the problem of child labor?

9. In the United States, why does child labor persist?

10. Why does the use of trade barriers to enforce standards abroad create concern for economists?

11. Describe the conclusion the chapter draws about whether countries use low standards to capture foreign markets and investment.

12. When practices are intolerable, what does your chapter suggest?

13. What does the International Labor Organization do?

14. Has the ILO played an important role to date? How likely is this to change in the future?

15. Is there one optimum environmental standard? Why? How might this make trade barriers less effective?

16. What lies at the root of labor and environmental issues?

17. What are the alternatives to trade measures to deal with differences in labor and environmental standards?

■ Just the Facts

1. Two or more economies (can, cannot) be deeply integrated if they have different rules, regulations, and standards governing their individual economies.

2. On a per capita basis, high-income countries generate more than _____ times the carbon dioxide of people living in low-income countries.

3. The amount of solid waste generated (rises, falls, is unchanged) as national income rises.

4. Child mortality rates (increase, decrease, are unchanged) as national income rises.

5. In low-income nations, _____ percent of children in the 10–14 age group are in the labor force. In low-middle income nations, the rate drops to _____ percent.

6. The International Labor Organization estimates that _____ children between the ages of five and 14 are working worldwide, and about _____ are working full time.

7. (Asia, Africa, Latin America) has about 61 percent of the children working, but (Asia, Africa, Latin America) had the highest percentage of its children working, an estimated 1 out of every 3 children.

8. Child labor is more common in (urban, suburban, rural) areas.

9. _____ of working children are employed in a family enterprise, often a _____.

10. Worldwide, most children work in activities that are oriented to (exports, domestic consumption).

11. The ILO estimates that _____ percent of working children are employed in export-oriented industries.

12. The use of child labor (rises, falls, is unchanged) as GDP increases. An estimated _____ to _____ percent of children five to 14 years of age work in countries with per capita GDPs less than $500 per person, while _____ to _____ percent of those children work in countries with per capita GDPs of $500 to $1,000.

13. Child labor is tied most strongly to _____ and _____.

14. The General Accounting Office of the U.S. government estimates that _____ children work in U.S. agriculture each year, and that this is probably an undercount. The United Farm Workers Union estimates that the true figure is closer to _____.

15. Currently there are _____ ILO conventions that are in force.

16. Of the eight core labor standards adopted by the ILO, the United States has ratified _____. _____ nations have ratified all eight.

■ Review Quiz

Check your mastery of the chapter by selecting the letter that gives the correct answer to each question.

1. Compared to high-income countries, low-income countries typically experience
    (a) lower wages and longer hours.
    (b) less safe working conditions.
    (c) dirtier industries and less regard for environmental degradation.
    (d) all of the above.

2. Which of the following is false?
    (a) When standards across countries vary by the level of development, it is better to have mutual recognition of standards or separate standards.
    (b) Differences in income are always an obstacle to the harmonization of standards.
    (c) It is sometimes unclear which country has the "best" rules.
    (d) Mutual recognition of standards may help clarify over time the costs and benefits of each.

3. Which of the following is false?
    (a) High-income countries generate more solid waste than low-income countries.
    (b) High-income countries generate more carbon dioxide emissions than low-income countries.
    (c) High-income countries experience more deforestation than low-income countries.
    (d) High-income countries have lower child mortality than low income-countries.

4. Which of the following is true?
    (a) Child labor is not a problem in the United States.
    (b) Child labor is most common in urban areas.
    (c) Estimates of child labor in Africa are that 1 out of 8 children under 14 are working.
    (d) Banning child labor would likely increase poverty for poor families.

5. Which of the following is not a core standard of the ILO?
   (a) Freedom of association and the right to collective bargaining
   (b) Elimination of forced labor
   (c) Creation of minimum wage laws
   (d) Effective abolition of child labor

6. The ILO
   (a) has been reluctant to use the full extent of its power.
   (b) has been especially supported by the United States, which was one of the first countries to ratify the eight core standards.
   (c) is likely to be less important in future negotiations about labor standards.
   (d) is a relatively new organization.

7. Trade sanctions as enforcement mechanisms for violating environmental standards
   (a) are likely to be very effective at lower costs than other policies.
   (b) are widely agreed on internationally since the core environmental problems and priorities have been identified.
   (c) are unlikely to start trade wars or trade disputes.
   (d) can create hazy boundaries between protectionism and concern for the environment.

8. An important difference between labor standards and environmental standards is that
   (a) poor labor conditions can be transboundary.
   (b) environmental problems can be transboundary.
   (c) environmental problems can be nontransboundary.
   (d) environmental problems have not been related to national income while low labor standards have been.

9. Which of the following is false?
   (a) The optimal set of environmental standards does not vary by nation.
   (b) It is impossible to identify any country that successfully competes for new investment on the basis of low environmental standards.
   (c) Stronger environmental standards raise production costs.
   (d) If environmental standards are correctly implemented, they raise national well being and lead to an economically optimal level of production.

10. Transboundary environmental problems
    (a) are likely to be solved by unilateral action by one nation.
    (b) may be the result of actions by many nations that lead to a global impact on an environmental resource.
    (c) always have a single low standard nation as the culprit or creator of the problem.
    (d) are located within the borders of a single nation.

■ Answers to Vocabulary

1. low-income country
2. lower-middle income country

3. upper-middle income country
4. high-income country
5. race to the bottom
6. harmonization of standards
7. mutual recognition of standards
8. separate standards
9. informal economy
10. International Labor Organization (ILO)
11. core labor standards
12. non-transboundary environmental problem
13. transboundary environmental problem
14. pollution haven

■ Answers to Chapter Review

1. First, national laws and regulations adopted for strictly domestic reasons unintentionally limit international commerce in a more integrated environment. Conflicts over standards are the second obstacle.

2. Disputes over technical product standards, health and safety standards, or labor and environmental standards. Adoption of a common set of standards gives a competitive advantage to firms that are already producing to that standard. Wide variation in world incomes means that economic conditions and living standards are vastly different between low-income and high-income countries.

3. With harmonization of standards, the nations create a mutually acceptable common standard. With mutual recognition of standards, each nation keeps its own standards but accepts the other nation's standard as equally valid and acceptable. With separate standards, each nation keeps its own standards and any products flowing into the nation must meet that nation's individual standards.

4. It creates a larger, more unified market and creates greater efficiency. If, however, an inferior standard is adopted, it might lock in place a less efficient solution and harm future development. It may also be difficult for low-income countries to have the administrative, scientific and technological capacity to design and enforce standards, much less have the same priorities as high-income countries.

5. Carbon dioxide emissions and solid waste both get worse as income rises; sanitation and water pollution get better. Other indicators are more mixed. Deforestation occurs more in low and upper middle income countries, while lower middle countries and high-income countries both experience reforestation. Air pollution initially gets worse as income rises, but at high income levels improves.

6. Child mortality and child labor both decrease as national income rises.

7. Prohibition of forced labor, freedom of association, the right to organize and to bargain collectively, an end to the exploitation of child labor, and nondiscrimination in employment

8. Child labor is a common family survival strategy, especially for farmers in rural areas where it is hard to enforce rules or to reach the poor with any supporting infrastructure or social services.

9. The main provisions of the U.S. labor code exempt agriculture from many of its standards, including those on child labor. Legislative reform has been difficult due to historical reasons, the seasonal nature of the work, the power of special interests, corruption, and official denial of the problem. The families are poor, live in rural areas, migrate with the harvest, and in other ways remain in a sector of the U.S. economy that is partially outside the coverage and the enforcement of the main protective standards.

10. Trade barriers are an expensive and grossly inefficient way to reach most of the goals for which they are used. Economists are not convinced that they create change in an exporting country's behavior; moreover they are concerned that the hazy borderline between protectionism and concern over standards is easily crossed, that nations lack agreement about the specific content of standards, and that imposing trade barriers over standards can lead to a wider trade war.

11. Empirical studies show that countries with low standards are less successful at attracting foreign investment. Low standards can reduce production costs, but they do not change a nation's comparative advantage. Nations that have similar comparative advantages could compete with each other using low standards, but this would not effect the high standard nations that have different comparative advantages. Low standards are highly correlated with low labor skills and low infrastructure, both of which create higher production costs and more than offset any savings from the low standards.

12. Moral issues make it unreasonable to rely solely on economic analysis, but the more united the world is against a particular inhumane labor practice, the more likely sanctions are to succeed.

13. It develops labor standards that are embodied in specific conventions and recommendations and encourages member nations to ratify those conventions. The ILO can receive formal complaints that a government is not enforcing core labor rights and investigate. If a nation is found to not be complying with ILO recommendations, the ILO can propose sanctions. The ILO also provides technical assistance to member nations in all aspects of labor policy.

14. The ILO has been a weak organization. The ILO has been reluctant to take action against violating nations. Not all members support it. Recently, it has received new support from a number of countries and is being viewed as a mechanism for resolving tensions between trade and labor issues.

15. No; because differences in income and preferences make the ideal standards vary by country. Budgets and regulatory efforts are not unlimited and the pressing problems and environmental resources that need protection are not the same. Countries will likely have different priorities. If one nation tries to impose its standards on another, this may actually reduce global well being. If resources and opportunities are different, so are the opportunity costs. One answer doesn't fit all.

16. Decisions about production and consumption, not trade

17. Labeling or certification for exports, requiring home country firms to follow home country standards whenever they open foreign operations, and increasing international negotiation

■ Answers to Just the Facts

1. can
2. 12
3. rises
4. decrease
5. 18; 6
6. 250 million; 120 million

7. Asia; Africa
8. rural
9. Three-fourths; subsistence farm
10. domestic consumption.
11. less than 6 to 7 percent
12. falls; 30; 60; 10; 30
13. poverty; agriculture
14. 300,000; 800,000
15. 157
16. 2; 97

■ Answers to Review Quiz

1. D
2. B
3. C
4. D
5. C
6. A
7. D
8. B
9. A
10. B

Chapter 9
Trade and the Balance of Payments

■ Vocabulary

For each numbered description, write in the correct term from the list provided.

capital account
current account
current account balance
debt service
external debt
financial account
foreign direct investment (FDI)
foreign portfolio investment
gross domestic product
gross national product (GNP)
international investment position
investment income
national income and product accounts
odious debt
official reserve assets
statistical discrepancy
technology transfer
trade balance
unilateral transfers

1. Records some specialized types of relatively small capital flows _____

2. The difference between exports and imports of goods and services _____

3. Records the flow of goods, services, income, and gifts into and out of the country _____

4. Records the flow of financial capital _____

5. Measures all current non-financial transactions between a nation and the rest of the world in goods, services, income, and gifts or transfers _____

6. Income received from investment abroad or income paid to foreigners on their domestic investments; can be thought of as payments for the use of another nation's financial capital _____

7. Any foreign aid or transfers received from foreigners or given to foreigners _____

8. The amount of mismeasurement in the balance of payments _____

9. New technologies, management techniques or ideas that come to a host country through capital inflows _____

10. The market value of all final goods and services produced in a given time period by the labor, capital, and resources of a country, regardless of where production occurred _____

11. The currencies of the largest and most stable economies of the world plus gold and special drawing rights _____

12. Purchases of tangible items such as real estate, factories, warehouses, transportation facilities, and other physical assets _____

13. Debt incurred without the consent of the people and that was not used for their benefit _____

14. Purchases of foreign stocks, bonds, and loans _____

15. The total of all foreign assets owned by residents of the home country minus the total of all domestic assets owned by foreigners _____

16. The internal, domestic accounting system used by countries to keep track of total production and total income _____

17. The market value of all final goods and services produced in a given time period within a nation's borders _____

18. Required interest and principle payments on outstanding loans _____

19. The total of all outstanding loans from abroad _____

■ Chapter Review

Answer the questions in the space provided below each.

1. How are the international transactions of a nation divided?

2. What items are recorded in the trade balance?

3. What is the difference between the trade balance and the current account balance?

4. What are the three components of the current account?

5. Why are governments concerned about financial flows?

6. In the financial crises of the last decade, what has been the common pattern for financial flows?

7. What pattern of borrowing has been particularly problematic in the case of a financial crisis? Why?

8. How has regulation of financial flows changed over recent years? Why did economists think the change would be helpful?

9. What has changed recently to cause economists and government officials to reconsider controls on financial flows?

10. What characteristics did the Mexican sexenio crises share?

11. What did President Zedillo do to avoid another sexenio crisis in 2000?

12. The difference between GNP and GDP is equal to which parts of the balance of payments?

13. Write the equation that summarizes the important relationship between the current account balance, investment, and public and private savings in the economy.

14. Why is domestic investment critical?

15. What is the general relationship between saving and investment and why does your text say it is imperfect?

16. How might a current account deficit be regarded as beneficial for the economy?

17. What problems might result from current account deficits?

18. When is taking on more debt helpful to an economy?

19. When is taking on more debt harmful to an economy?

20. What problems does excessive debt service create?

21. What indicators are used to classify debt as excessive?

22. How do countries qualify for debt-relief under the Highly Indebted Poor Countries effort?

23. What are the primary arguments against debt relief?

24. What final costs and benefits of capital inflows does the chapter address?

■ Just the Facts

1. In 2002 the United States purchased _____ in goods and services from foreign suppliers and exported _____ and had a trade balance of _____.

2. A trade deficit occurs when exports of goods and services are (greater than, less than, equal to) imports of goods and services.

3. For the United States in 2002, the balance on goods was a (deficit, surplus, zero) and the balance on services was a (deficit, surplus, zero).

4. Services were _____ percent of total U.S. exports in 2002 and for many years have been a (growing, shrinking, stable) part of U.S. and world trade.

5. The most commonly cited measurement of a nation's transactions with the rest of the world is its _____.

6. A debit item is entered into the balance of payments as a (positive, negative) number and a credit item is entered into the balance of payments as a (positive, negative) number.

7. Income received is a (debit, credit) item in the (current account, financial account, capital account).

8. Large deficits in the U.S. current account have been a more or less constant feature of the U.S. economy since _____.

9. The capital and financial accounts data are (flow, stock) variables. The data are presented as (net, gross) figures.

10. Outflows of financial assets are a (debit, credit) item while inflows are a (debit, credit) item.

11. Looking at the financial account data, it is (possible, not possible) to determine the total amount of official reserve assets available to a nation.

12. _____ are equivalent to reserve assets for foreign governments.

13. Direct foreign investment items have (more, less, similar) liquidity to foreign portfolio investment items.

14. In most of the financial crises of the last decade, there were large and sudden _____ as both home and foreign investors tried to avoid the expected crises.

15. Until recently, nations limited financial flows that were related to transactions in the (current account, financial account, capital account).

16. A _____ is a Mexican word for the single six-year term served by its presidents.

17. If government budgets are in deficit, there will be (more, less, a similar amount of) investment spending than there would have been had government budgets been in surplus.

18. Another name for the current account balance is _____.

19. If the current account is in surplus, domestic national saving finances the purchases of domestic goods by (foreign, domestic) users of those goods.

20. In 2002, the current account deficit for the United States was nearly _____ percent of GNP.

21. In 2001, 138 developing countries classified as low- and middle-income by the World Bank had external debts that totaled _____ U.S. dollars, most of which were owed directly by the developing country governments or were guaranteed by them.

22. The large current account deficits of the 1980s, 1990s, and 2000s have eroded the United States investment position from _____ in 1983 to _____ in 1989 to _____ in 2001.

■ For Practice

1. The following data is from the U.S. Bureau of Economic Analysis and is for the U.S. economy for the first quarter of 2004 and is in millions of dollars.

Exports of goods	193,920
Exports of services	82,918
Investment income received	84,479
Imports of goods	344,688
Imports of services	69,081
Investment income paid	71,804
Net unilateral transfers	20,623

   Given the data, for each of the following questions, calculate the appropriate balance:
   (a) The balance on goods
   (b) The balance on services
   (c) The trade balance
   (d) The balance on income
   (e) The current account balance

2. For each of the following, state whether the item would be entered as a debit or a credit and whether it would be a current account item or a financial account item.

A	unilateral transfers received from foreigners	—
B	imports of services	—
C	direct investment abroad	—
D	foreign purchases of domestic stocks and bonds	—
E	exports of merchandise	—
F	foreign official assets in domestic economy	—
G	unilateral transfers given to foreigners	—
H	exports of services	—
I	income received	—
J	domestic purchases of foreign stocks and bonds	—
K	foreign direct investment in the domestic economy	—
L	income paid	—
M	imports of merchandise	—

3. Use the following data from the U.S. Bureau of Economic Analysis for the U.S. economy for 2003 to answer the questions below. All figures are in millions of U.S. dollars.

Net change in the capital account	–3,079
Statistical discrepancy	–12,012
Net unilateral transfers	–67,439
Imports of services	256,337
Net change in U.S. official reserve assets	1,523
Exports of goods	713,122
Net change in U.S. government nonreserve assets	537
Income received	294,385
Net change in U.S. private assets	–285,474
Exports of services	307,381
Net change in foreign official assets in U.S.	248,573
Income paid	261,106
Net change in private foreign assets in U.S.	580,600
Imports of goods	1,260,674

(a) What is the trade balance?
(b) What is the current account balance?
(c) What is the financial account balance?
(d) Check to see that current account + capital account + financial account + statistical discrepancy = 0.

Review Quiz

Check your mastery of the chapter by selecting the letter that gives the correct answer to each question.

1. If U.S. mutual funds invest in the Mexican stock market,
   (a) the initial stock purchase would be recorded in the income component in the U.S. current account.
   (b) the flow of dividends back to the mutual fund in the United States would count as income paid in Mexico's current account.
   (c) the flow of dividends back to the mutual fund in the United States would count as income paid in the U.S. current account.
   (d) the flow of dividends back to the mutual fund in the United States would count as a credit in the U.S. financial account.

2. One of the primary differences between foreign direct investment (FDI) and foreign portfolio investment is
   (a) FDI makes a claim on future output of the foreign country where foreign portfolio investment does not.
   (b) FDI is recorded as a credit item and portfolio investment is a debit item.
   (c) FDI is regarded as having a longer time horizon than portfolio investment.
   (d) FDI is more liquid than portfolio investment.

3. If a nation's exports of goods and services are smaller than its imports of goods and services,
   (a) its trade balance will be in surplus.
   (b) its trade balance will be in deficit.
   (c) its trade in services must be greater than its trade in goods.
   (d) trade is clearly not benefiting this nation.

4. Which of the following is not an explanation for consistent deficits in the U.S. current account over the last twenty plus years?
   (a) Rapid economic growth in the U.S. raised incomes.
   (b) When national income rises, demand for imports rises as well.
   (c) U.S. trading partners were experiencing rapid economic growth.
   (d) Foreign demand for U.S. exports grew less rapidly than U.S. demand for imports.

5. Which of the following is false?
   (a) Current account deficits are a sign of current economic weakness for the United States.
   (b) Current account deficits are not sustainable in the long run.
   (c) Current account deficits have the potential to create serious future problems.
   (d) Current account deficits mean that the financial account is in surplus.

6. Which of the following is true?
   (a) If U.S. stockholders receive dividend checks on their ownership of shares in a foreign corporation, that would be recorded in the U.S. balance of payments as a change in U.S. private assets abroad.
   (b) Financial capital sent to Guatemala to build a factory would count as a current account item.
   (c) Investment income items in the current account are movements of investment capital from one nation to another.
   (d) Investment income flows are payments for the use of another nation's financial capital.

7. Which of the following statements is correct?
   (a) Income received would be a debit item in the current account.
   (b) Purchases of foreign stocks and bonds would be a credit in the financial account.
   (c) Sending home wages to family members abroad would be a debit item to unilateral transfers.
   (d) Exports of services would be a debit item in the current account.

8. Which of the following is correct?
   (a) Purchases of foreign assets by U.S. citizens require capital outflows and are counted as debit entries into the U.S. financial account.
   (b) Purchases of foreign assets by U.S. citizens require capital inflows and are counted as debit entries into the U.S. financial account.
   (c) Purchases of foreign assets by U.S. citizens require capital outflows and are counted as credit entries into the U.S. financial account.
   (d) When foreigners purchase U.S. assets, there is a capital outflow and a debit entry into the U.S. financial account.

9. Which of the following is false?
   (a) In most countries, the bulk of financial flows is private.
   (b) Financial flows are often vehicles for transmitting a financial crisis from one nation to others.
   (c) Financial flows are not a major concern for governments, but are for private investors.
   (d) Some financial flows are very mobile and can introduce volatility into an economy.

10. Which of the following is not correct about reserve assets?
    (a) They are used to settle international debts.
    (b) Central banks and treasury ministries use them as a store of value.
    (c) They play an important role in international finance.
    (d) When they become more abundant, it signals serious problems for the nation accumulating the reserve assets.

11. Which of the following is false? In late 1994 and early 1995,
    (a) Mexico owed dollars to various international investors.
    (b) a sudden outflow of dollars from Mexico during 1994 reduced the supply of dollars in Mexico.
    (c) the outflow of dollars made it impossible for Mexico to pay its international bills in the short run.
    (d) Mexico was able to replenish its reserve assets by selling its oil.

12. Other things unchanged, countries that have
    (a) high rates of saving have low rates of domestic investment.
    (b) budget surpluses have higher rates of domestic investment.
    (c) budget deficits have higher rates of domestic investment.
    (d) low rates of saving have high rates of domestic investment.

13. Current account surpluses
    (a) mean that domestic savings are flowing abroad.
    (b) mean that foreign savings are flowing into the domestic economy.
    (c) will not affect the rate of foreign investment by the domestic economy.
    (d) mean foreigners are investing more in the domestic economy than domestic investors are sending abroad.

14. Which of the following is false?
    (a) The general public and the media often interpret a current account deficit as a sign of weakness and as harmful to the nation's welfare.
    (b) A current account deficit allows more investment than would be possible otherwise.
    (c) More investment is associated with higher living standards.
    (d) Current account deficits indicate that foreigners do not feel confident about the domestic economy.

∎ Answers to Vocabulary

1. capital account
2. trade balance
3. current account
4. financial account
5. current account balance
6. investment income
7. unilateral transfers
8. statistical discrepancy
9. technology transfer
10. gross national product (GNP)
11. official reserve assets
12. foreign direct investment (FDI)
13. odious debt
14. foreign portfolio investment
15. international investment position
16. national income and product accounts
17. gross domestic product
18. debt service
19. external debt

Answers to Chapter Review

1. Into three separate accounts called the current account, the capital account, and the financial account. The current account records flows of goods and services, the financial account flows of financial capital, and the capital account some other types of capital flows.

2. Exports of goods and services minus imports of goods and services.

3. The trade balance is a component of the current account balance, which is a much more comprehensive measurement of current, non-financial transactions between a nation and the rest of the world

4. The trade balance (exports of goods and services minus imports of goods and services), the balance on investment income, and the balance of unilateral transfers.

5. All forms of international debts are settled with reserve assets and so the increase or loss in these assets plays an important role in the government's and the business community's ability to conduct their activities. Some financial flows are very mobile and can change rapidly in the short run. This introduces volatility into the domestic economy and may cause financial problems to spread rapidly from one nation to others.

6. Large and sudden financial outflows, particularly of portfolio investment, have occurred as both foreign and home investors tried to move their assets out of the country. This drains the nation of most of its reserve assets and puts further downward pressure on the currency.

7. Borrowing abroad in reserve currencies to lend at home in the national currency has been particularly damaging because the payments are made in the collapsing home currency but the debts have to be repaid in the rising reserve currencies, making banks' income streams inadequate to service their international debts.

8. Most nations used to regulate and limit financial flows to transactions related to the current account. There has recently been a significant lifting of controls on financial flows across international boundaries. The restrictions had limited the availability of financial capital, and it was also difficult to disentangle financial flows related to the current account from financial flows related strictly to the financial account. Freeing financial flows potentially could reduce costs, increase efficiency, and encourage more investment and growth.

9. Extreme volatility in some financial markets has caused severe damage to a number of countries. At this point, there is not much agreement on how to get the benefits of increased investment while minimizing the risk of capital flight.

10. They were characterized by large and sudden outflows of financial capital, by rapid outflows of official reserve assets such as U.S. dollars, and by a relatively large inflow of short-term debt caused by previous large financial inflows. All but the 1988 crisis also were characterized by a significantly overvalued peso and a large current account deficit.

11. He reduced the reliance of Mexican investors on foreign financing by encouraging domestic saving. He encouraged foreign direct investment rather than portfolio investment. He balanced the government budget. He arranged emergency lines of credit in case a crisis did occur. He moved the country from a controlled value of the peso to a market-based system.

12. The investment income and the unilateral transfers components of the current account

13. $S + (G - T) = I + CA$

14. New investments in machinery and equipment are a source of economic growth. It is essential in order to upgrade the skills of the labor force, to provide new capital, and to improve the quality of production by introducing new technology.

15. In general, investment rises as savings rise so high savings countries have more investment than low savings countries. But government budgets and the current account moderate this relationship so it is not one-to-one.

16. The deficit enables more investment in the economy and investment increases living standards. Capital inflows in general indicate foreign confidence in the domestic economy.

17. Capital inflows increase the stock of foreign-owned assets in the home country, raising the possibility that a future change in foreign investor expectations could lead to capital flight. Capital flight can lead to a depletion of international reserves and a financial crisis.

18. When the borrowed funds are used to increase skills and production levels, the increase in output will allow the borrower to service the loan without difficulty.

19. If the borrowed funds do not contribute to an expansion of the nation's productive capabilities, debt service becomes an unsustainable burden that holds back economic development. This might happen due to corruption, inefficiency, changes in demand for a key product, natural disasters, politics, or lender behavior.

20. Because debt service can take up an increasingly greater part of the overall budget, it can hurt the government's ability to fund other items in the budget and limit the amount of resources available to invest in economic development. It can also intensify and spread a crisis.

21. Debt divided by exports of goods and services and debt divided by gross national product

22. Based on their level of poverty, a good track record of reform, and a high level of external debt relative to exports

23. Countries with large foreign debts may be poorly administered. Forgiving debts just leads to new rounds of borrowing that restores debt to the previous level. Debt relief for some countries may encourage others to borrow excessively in hope that their debts will also be forgiven.

24. On the benefit side, technology transfer; on the cost side, the fact that capital inflows provide access to political power and in some countries there may be few checks on the power of wealth.

■ Answers to Just the Facts

1. $1,392 billion; $974 billion; –$418 billion
2. less than
3. deficit; surplus
4. 30; growing
5. trade balance
6. negative; positive
7. credit; current account
8. 1982
9. flow; net
10. debit; credit

11. not possible
12. U.S. treasury securities
13. less
14. financial outflows
15. financial account
16. sexenio
17. less
18. net foreign investment
19. foreign
20. 4.7
21. 2,332.1 billion
22. $288.6 billion; 0; –$2,315 billion

■ Answers to For Practice

1. (a) –150,768
   (b) 13,837
   (c) –136,931
   (d) 12,675
   (e) –144,879

2.
A	unilateral transfers received from foreigners	credit, current
B	imports of services	debit, current
C	direct investment abroad	debit, financial
D	foreign purchases of domestic stocks and bonds	credit, financial
E	exports of merchandise	credit, current
F	foreign official assets in domestic economy	credit, financial
G	unilateral transfers given to foreigners	debit, current
H	exports of services	credit, current
I	income received	credit, current
J	domestic purchases of foreign stocks and bonds	debit, financial
K	foreign direct investment in the domestic economy	credit, financial
L	income paid	debit, current
M	imports of merchandise	debit, current

3. (a) –496,508
   (b) –530,668
   (c) 545,759

■ Answers to Review Quiz

1. B
2. C
3. B
4. C
5. A
6. D
7. C
8. A
9. C
10. D
11. D
12. B
13. A
14. D

Chapter 10
Exchange Rates and Exchange Rate Systems

■ Vocabulary

For each numbered description, write in the correct term from the list provided.

appreciation	exchange rate risk	managed float
Bretton Woods exchange rate system	fixed exchange rate system	nominal exchange rate
Convertibility Law	flexible (floating) exchange rate	optimal currency area
covered interest arbitrage	forward exchange rate	pegged exchange rate
crawling peg	forward market	purchasing power parity
currency board	gold standard	real exchange rate
depreciation	hedging	Smithsonian agreement
dollarization	interest rate arbitrage	spot market
exchange rate	interest parity	

1. The price of one currency stated in terms of a second currency _____

2. When a currency buys more units of another currency _____

3. When a currency buys fewer units of another currency _____

4. Holding foreign exchange to take advantage of differences in interest rates _____

5. The fact that currencies constantly change value creates uncertainty about the value of future payments to be made or to be received _____

6. The price of a currency that will be delivered in the future _____

7. The market where currencies for future delivery are bought and sold _____

8. The market for buying and selling currencies in the present _____

9. Using forward markets and/or options to protect from exchange rate risk while holding financial assets denominated in foreign currencies _____

10. When interest arbitrageurs use the forward market to insure against exchange rate risk _____

11. Theory stating that the equilibrium value of an exchange rate is the level that allows a given amount of money to buy the same quantity of goods abroad that it will buy at home _____

12. Market or nominal exchange rate adjusted for price differences _____

13. The value of a nation's money is defined in terms of a fixed amount of a commodity such as gold or in terms of a fixed amount of another currency _____

14. Current market exchange rate _____

15. The value of a nation's currency in terms of other nations' currencies is allowed to vary in response to market forces _____

16. A form of fixed exchange rates where nations keep gold as an international reserve and are prepared to exchange their currencies for a set amount of gold _____

17. A fixed exchange rate system developed at the end of World War II that lasted until the early 1970s _____

18. A fixed exchange rate system that uses another currency (rather than gold) to anchor the value of the home currency _____

19. A fixed exchange rate system that is periodically adjusted _____

20. Countries claim to have floating exchange rates, but they intervene occasionally by buying and selling their currency to adjust the exchange rate _____

21. The adoption of the U.S. dollar as the country's own currency _____

22. Law that fixed the value of the Argentine peso to the U.S. dollar at a one-to-one rate _____

23. Oversees the exchange rate system and enforces the fixed exchange rate _____

24. The major industrialized countries agreed to devalue the gold content of the U.S. dollar _____

25. Two or more countries that would be better off economically by sharing a currency rather than maintaining their own national money _____

26. Theory stating that the difference between any pair of countries' interest rates is approximately equal to the expected change in the exchange rate _____

■ Chapter Review

Answer the questions in the space provided below each.

1. Why is there so much debate about the selection and management of a country's exchange rate system?

   _____

2. Why do people hold foreign currencies?

   _____

3. How do interest rate arbitrageurs make money and what function do they perform for the global economy?

4. How do foreign currency speculators make money and what function do they perform for the global economy?

5. Who are the four main participants in foreign exchange markets? Which is the most important?

6. Why are firms that do business in more than one country subject to exchange rate risk? What solution was created in the 19th century to deal with this risk?

7. What factors affect the exchange rate in the long run?

8. What are some of the unrealistic assumptions of purchasing power parity?

9. What factors affect exchange rates in the medium run?

10. What factors affect exchange rates in the short run?

11. What is the interest rate parity condition?

12. What happens when the percentage difference in the forward and spot rates is insufficient to compensate for higher interest rates in the home country?

13. Why is the real exchange rate important?

14. What is the potential macroeconomic problem with an appreciation in the real exchange rate for a nation's currency?

15. What are the three rules for maintaining a gold exchange standard?

16. What is a pegged exchange rate standard? What is the main potential problem and how is it avoided?

17. What is the problem with differences in inflation rates for nations that are using pegged exchange rates? How is this problem addressed?

18. What has research shown about the connection between the choice of an exchange rate system and a nation's inflation or economic growth rates?

19. If the goal of nations is to minimize shocks to their economy, which type of exchange rate system should they choose?

20. What is the most important issue in choosing an exchange rate system?

21. Why might a group of countries want to share a common currency?

22. What are the four conditions for adopting a single currency identified in the chapter?

■ Just the Facts

1. To get the exchange rates posted in the financial press, you would have to purchase _____ in currency.

2. Foreign exchange policies are (easier, more difficult) for economists to agree on than trade policies.

3. _____ are the most important participants in foreign exchange markets.

4. Purchasing power parity influences currency values (directly, indirectly).

5. The daily volume of foreign exchange transactions in the world's currency markets was around _____ in 2001.

6. Between 1989 and 1998, the daily volume of currency transactions grew _____ percent per year.

7. The adoption of the euro led to (an increase, a decrease, no change) in the daily volume of currency transactions.

8. In 2001, _____ percent of every trade involved the U.S. dollar as either the currency sold or bought.

9. _____ is the largest center of currency trading.

10. If the forward rate is greater than the spot rate, it signals that the markets expect the home currency to (appreciate, depreciate, be unchanged) over the maturity period of the forward rate.

11. If inflation is higher in the home market, then the real value of the home currency (appreciates, depreciates, is unchanged).

12. By the end of the 20th century, (flexible exchange rates, fixed exchange rates, gold standards) were the norm in every region of the world.

13. About _____ of all the U.S. dollars in circulation are outside the United States.

14. In March _____, major currencies began to float against each other and the Bretton Woods system was over.

■ For practice

Calculate the answers for the problems below.

1. For each of the following, state what will happen in the foreign exchange market for Mexican pesos.
   (a) U.S. nominal interest rates rise.
   (b) Mexican products become more popular in the United States.
   (c) The market expects a future depreciation in the Mexican peso.
   (d) Mexican inflation rates are higher than U.S. inflation rates.
   (e) Mexicans want to consume more U.S. goods and services.

2. Assume $i = 10$, $i^* = 11$ percent, and $R = \$1.00$. In order for the interest parity condition to hold, what is the appropriate forward rate for the period that matches the interest rate periods?

3. If the current exchange rate for euros is $1.20, the price index for the European Union is 150 and the price index for the United States is 100, what is the real exchange rate? Which currency is likely to depreciate in the future?

■ Review Quiz

Check your mastery of the chapter by selecting the letter that gives the correct answer to each question.

1. Which of the following is false?
   (a) Exchange rates posted by the financial press are wholesale rather than retail.
   (b) In order to realize the exchange rate listed, a bank or currency trader has to purchase large quantities of a currency, typically a million dollars or more.
   (c) Tourists can typically get foreign exchange at the rates posted in the financial press.
   (d) Most exchange rates are in a state of constant change.

2. Speculators
   (a) need the currency to buy or sell products.
   (b) prefer currencies that are unlikely to change in value.
   (c) often help to bring currencies into equilibrium after they have become over-valued or undervalued.
   (d) have a very good reputation with the public and the media.

3. Which of the following is true?
   (a) An increase in the demand for U.S. dollars would cause the dollar to depreciate.
   (b) An increase in the supply of U.S. dollars would cause the dollar to appreciate.
   (c) A decrease in the demand for U.S. dollars would cause the dollar to appreciate.
   (d) A decrease in the supply of U.S. dollars would cause the dollar to appreciate.

4. As the pound depreciates against the U.S. dollar,
   (a) more people from the United Kingdom will want to buy U.S. goods.
   (b) British goods become less expensive for U.S. consumers.
   (c) U.S. consumers will want to buy less products from the United Kingdom.
   (d) the U.S. dollar also depreciates.

5. Which of the following is true?
   (a) The NAFTA nations would make an ideal single currency area because their business cycles are highly synchronized.
   (b) Mexico would not gain anything from dollarization.
   (c) There is a high degree of consensus that the NAFTA nations should integrate beyond the free trade area level.
   (d) Some Mexicans support dollarization for their economy.

6. If $i = 0.1$ and $i^* = 0.12$ and $R = 1.00$, what would F equal for the interest rate parity condition to hold?
   (a) .90
   (b) 1.00
   (c) 1.10
   (d) 1.20

7. If Mexican pesos currently trade for $0.10, the Mexican price index is 250 and the U.S. price index is 125, which of the following is false?
   (a) U.S. goods are more expensive for Mexican businesses and consumers in real terms when they trade pesos at the nominal exchange rate.
   (b) The real exchange rate for pesos is $0.20.
   (c) Mexican goods and services are more expensive for U.S. businesses and consumers in real terms when they trade dollars at the nominal exchange rate.
   (d) In real terms, the peso has appreciated and the dollar has depreciated.

8. Suppose Costa Rica pegs its exchange rate to the U.S. dollar. Which of the following is true?
   (a) If the U.S. dollar appreciates against the euro, this could hurt Costa Rica's European tourism business.
   (b) If the U.S. dollar appreciates against other major currencies, this could hurt Costa Rica's U.S. tourism business.
   (c) If U.S. and Costa Rican inflation rates are similar, the peg could create problems.
   (d) If a crawling peg is used appropriately, the real exchange rate for dollars in Costa Rica will decline over time.

9. Dollarization
   (a) has not occurred anywhere in the world.
   (b) is extremely popular and embraced widely around the world.
   (c) means that countries give up any ability to influence their exchange rate.
   (d) is illegal internationally so it must be done informally rather than formally.

10. Which of the following did not occur under the Bretton Woods system?
    (a) The U.S. economy grew at a different rate than the economies of its trading partners.
    (b) U.S. prices rose relative to foreign prices, causing the real exchange rate to appreciate.
    (c) The U.S. devalued its nominal exchange rate selectively, against only a few currencies, creating animosity.
    (d) The dollars accumulated outside the United States exceeded the U.S. supply of gold.

11. Which of the following is true?
    (a) Using a single currency creates uncertainty about prices for the participating countries.
    (b) Using a single currency reduces the price effects of currency market speculation on trade between the countries.
    (c) Adopting a common currency may make developing countries look less credible.
    (d) Adopting a common currency increases transaction costs.

12. Which of the following is false?
    (a) If a country tends to have shocks to its economy that come from its monetary sector, a fixed exchange rate system may be better.
    (b) Flexible exchange rate systems are better able to help a nation adopt to shocks that originate outside the domestic economy.
    (c) Fixed exchange rates are able to act as a buffer between the domestic economy and the outside world.
    (d) Countries that have a high degree of dependence on a single, major economy tend to peg their currencies to that currency.

■ Answers to Vocabulary

1. exchange rate
2. appreciation
3. depreciation
4. interest rate arbitrage
5. exchange rate risk
6. forward exchange rate
7. forward market
8. spot market
9. hedging
10. covered interest arbitrage
11. purchasing power parity
12. real exchange rate
13. fixed exchange rate system
14. nominal exchange rate
15. flexible (floating) exchange rate
16. gold standard

17. Bretton Woods exchange rate system
18. pegged exchange rate
19. crawling peg
20. managed float
21. dollarization
22. Convertibility Law
23. currency board
24. Smithsonian agreement
25. optimal currency area
26. interest parity

■ Answers to Chapter Review

1. Countries have to decide on the type of exchange rate system they desire, ranging from flexible to fixed; each type of system requires different government policies; and each type of system responds differently to pressures from the world economy. All of the possible interactions make it difficult to predict outcomes and hard to reach consensus on an optimal set of choices.

2. For trade and investment, to take advantage of differences in interest rates between markets, and to speculate.

3. They acquire money where interest rates are relatively low and lend it where rates are relatively high, making a return on the differential in interest rates. By moving financial capital this way, they keep interest rates from diverging too far by raising rates in the low interest rate country due to their demand for funds and lowering rates in the high interest country by supplying funds. The drawing together of interest rates is one way in which economic conditions are transmitted across national borders and forms a primary linkage between national economies.

4. They hold foreign currencies that they expect to appreciate and sell foreign currencies that they expect to depreciate. They may bring exchange rates for currencies back into equilibrium through their buying and selling after a period of over- or undervaluation. If they are wrong about valuations, they lose money and go out of business. But their actions may also move currencies away from their optimal values and cause problems for the nations involved, so they remain controversial.

5. retail customers, commercial banks, foreign exchange brokers, and central banks, with commercial banks being the most important

6. There is uncertainty about the exact costs and revenues the firm will receive in the future as the currencies fluctuate against each other. When the contract is signed, one amount may be expected and when the payment arrives and is switched into the domestic currency, a different amount may result given fluctuating exchange rates. Forward currency markets were created so a firm could lock in a future exchange rate the day that the contract is signed for the exchange of goods and services. The forward market contract guarantees a set price for the foreign currency, often months in the future.

7. In the long run, the theory of purchasing power parity indicates that differences in inflation rates will have a big effect on the exchange rate. In essence, the same basket of products should cost the same in each country, taking the exchange rate into account. When these prices differ, there should be resulting changes in the exchange rate.

8. It fails to take into account transportation and other transactions costs or trade barriers. Not all goods can be traded internationally.

9. The business cycle within each nation dictates the strength of its economic expansion. Rapid growth means rising incomes, more consumption, and usually more imports and travel abroad. This tends to lead to a depreciating domestic currency. Slower growth tends to be associated with an appreciating domestic currency.

10. The flow of financial capital is the largest short run factor and it is very responsive to changes in interest rates and to expectations about future exchange rates.

11. The difference between interest rates in each nation is approximately equal to the expected change in exchange rates.

12. Financial capital will flow out of the foreign market into the home market, increasing the demand for the home currency and increasing the supply of the foreign currency, decreasing R and decreasing home interest rates due to the increased supply of financial capital to the home market.

13. Tourists and business people who use foreign exchange are most interested in the purchasing power they get when they convert, not the number of units of foreign currency.

14. There can be a build up in the nation's current account deficit over time and a potential collapse in the future value of the currency.

15. First, fix the value of the currency in terms of gold. Second, keep supply of currency fixed in a constant proportion to the supply of gold. Finally, stand ready and willing to accept currency in exchange for gold.

16. A nation fixes the value of its currency to another currency instead of to gold. It makes the home currency fluctuate against all other currencies at the same rate as the currency it has chosen as its peg. Pegs can be created to groups of currencies rather than to a single currency to avoid this problem.

17. If inflation rates are very different between the home country and the nation(s) it is using for the peg, this can lead to an appreciation in the real exchange rate and expectations for devaluation. Crawling pegs are periodically adjusted for differences in inflation rates. If correctly handled, the real exchange rate remains constant.

18. At this point, no conclusions can be drawn. It used to be that fixed exchange rate systems had lower inflation and flexible systems higher growth, but recent studies seem to show that no particular system ranks above another in terms of its ability to provide superior macroeconomic results.

19. If shocks originate in the monetary sector, a fixed rate is better. If shocks come from the external environment, a flexible rate is better. Smaller countries that are open to the global economy seem to do better with flexible systems.

20. credibility and sustainability

21. It reduces transactions costs by reducing costs of doing conversions, simplifying accounting and bookkeeping, and enabling easier price comparisons across nations. It eliminates price fluctuations caused by changes in the exchange rate. It increases political trust and integration between nations. It may lead to greater credibility for the exchange rate system.

22. 1. Relatively similar macroeconomic conditions/synchronized business cycles. 2. High degree of labor and capital mobility. 3. Regional policies for addressing any imbalances that may result. 4. Seeking a level of integration that goes beyond trade.

■ Answers to Just the Facts

1. a million dollars or more
2. more difficult
3. commercial banks
4. indirectly
5. $1.2 trillion
6. 10
7. a decrease
8. 90
9. London
10. depreciate
11. appreciates
12. flexible exchange rates
13. 2/3
14. 1973

■ Answers to For practice

1. (a) The demand for pesos will fall and the supply of pesos will increase.
   (b) The demand for pesos will rise.
   (c) The demand for pesos will fall and the supply of pesos will increase.
   (d) The demand for pesos will fall and the supply of pesos will increase.
   (e) The supply of pesos will increase.
2. $1.10
3. $1.80. The euro is likely to depreciate in the future as Europeans take advantage of cheap prices in the United States and U.S. households and businesses find European products too expensive.

■ Answers to Review Quiz

1. C
2. C
3. D
4. B
5. D
6. D

7. A
8. A
9. C
10. C
11. B
12. C

Chapter 11
An Introduction to Open Economy Macroeconomics

■ Vocabulary

For each numbered description, write in the correct term from the list provided.

adjustment process
aggregate demand (AD)
aggregate supply (AS)
contractionary fiscal policy
contractionary monetary policy

expansionary fiscal policy
expansionary monetary policy
expenditure reducing policy
expenditure switching policy
fiscal policy

intermediate inputs
J-curve
monetary policy
multiplier effect
open market operations

1. An increase in the money supply and a fall in interest rates to raise national income _____

2. Goods purchased by one business from another to use in production _____

3. Increases in taxes and cuts in government spending to lower national income _____

4. When the first impact of a domestic currency depreciation on the current account is a further worsening rather than an improvement _____

5. When an original change in spending works its way through the economy, the change in total output is greater than the initial change in spending _____

6. A decrease in the money supply and an increase in interest rates to lower national income _____

7. Using government spending and taxes to change equilibrium output, employment or the price level _____

8. Total expenditure on final goods and services at various price levels _____

9. Contractionary fiscal or monetary policies that cut the overall level of demand in the economy _____

10. Using the money supply and interest rates to change equilibrium output, employment, or the price level _____

11. Cuts in taxes and increases in government spending to raise national income _____

12. The government buying and selling bonds to change the money supply _____

13. Changes in the trade deficit that are caused by a change in the exchange rate _____

14. Total output of final goods and services at various price levels _____

15. Policy changes that cause some consumer and firm spending to switch from foreign goods to domestic goods _____

■ Chapter Review

Answer the questions in the space provided below each.

1. What role do national governments take in the macroeconomy?

2. What is the fundamental identity in the macroeconomy?

3. What is the significance of the three parts of the aggregate supply curve?

4. Describe the possible changes that could shift aggregate demand.

5. How could economic growth be shown using the aggregate demand/aggregate supply model?

6. What is the multiplier effect?

7. As income and spending rises, what happens to imports?

8. What is the difference between fiscal and monetary policies?

9. What are the potential drawbacks of using fiscal policy?

10. What is the most frequently used tool for monetary policy?

11. Which U.S. federal programs were created as a result of the Great Depression?

12. How did policy making impact the Great Depression in the United States?

13. What is the relationship between interest rates and the exchange rate?

14. What effect does expansionary monetary policy have on a nation's currency? Why?

15. What is the downside to using contractionary monetary policy to solve a rapid depreciation in a currency?

16. How does fiscal policy affect the exchange rate?

17. Which type of expansionary policy has a more robust effect on national income? Which type of expansionary policy has an unambiguous effect on the current account? Why?

18. In the long run, what restores balance to the purchasing power of national currencies?

19. What types of things must policies aimed at correcting a current account deficit do within the economy?

20. Why are expenditure reducing policies necessary?

21. Why are expenditure switching policies necessary?

22. Does an exchange rate depreciation lead to an immediate change in spending on exports and imports?

23. What are the main differences between the U.S. current account deficits of the 1980s and the 1990s?

24. What are some of the obstacles to macroeconomic policy coordination internationally?

■ Just the Facts

1. Expansionary fiscal policy shifts aggregate demand to the (left, right) by (increasing, decreasing) government spending or (increasing, decreasing) taxes.

2. Contractionary fiscal policy involves (increasing, decreasing) taxes or (increasing, decreasing) government spending to shift aggregate (demand, supply) to the (right, left).

3. If the central bank wants more investment spending to occur in the economy, it (buys, sells) bonds to (increase, decrease) cash reserves in the financial system and to (raise, lower) interest rates.

4. Contractionary monetary policy would lead to (higher, lower) interest rates and (more, less) total spending in the economy.

5. In the United States by 1933, over _____ percent of the labor force was unemployed and real GDP had fallen by nearly _____ percent.

6. Two recessions occurred in the 1930s in the United States. The first lasted from _____ to _____ and second began in _____ and ended in _____.

7. An increase in interest rates causes that nation to experience an (inflow, outflow) of financial capital and causes its currency to (appreciate, depreciate).

8. A common response to stop a depreciation of a currency is to use (expansionary, contractionary) (fiscal, monetary) policy, which could lead to (inflation, a recession).

9. Expansionary fiscal policy leads to (more, less) imports than expansionary monetary policy.

10. The exchange rate effect of contractionary fiscal policy causes (imports, exports) to fall and (diminishes, enhances) the contractionary effects of the policy.

11. The effects of fiscal policy on the current account are (definite, indeterminate), and the effects of monetary policy on the current account are (definite, indeterminate).

12. In practice, the most dangerous imbalance are large (financial, capital, currrent) account (deficits, surpluses).

13. In the United States there is a median lag of _____ months before a change in the exchange rate begins to affect exports and median lag of more than _____ months for imports.

■ Review Quiz

Check your mastery of the chapter by selecting the letter that gives the correct answer to each question.

1. Which of the following would shift aggregate demand to the left?
   (a) an increase in government spending
   (b) an increase in taxes
   (c) an increase in investment spending
   (d) an increase in economic growth

2. Economic growth would be shown in the model as
   (a) a rightward shift of aggregate supply.
   (b) a rightward shift of aggregate demand.
   (c) a leftward shift of aggregate demand.
   (d) a leftward shift of aggregate supply.

3. Which of the following correctly identifies a policy tool?
   (a) Contractionary fiscal policy calls for increasing government spending.
   (b) Expansionary monetary policy calls for tax cuts.
   (c) Expansionary fiscal policy calls for increasing the money supply.
   (d) Contractionary monetary policy calls for raising interest rates.

4. Which of the following is false?
   (a) U.S. output never grew during the 1930s.
   (b) The Great Depression was made up of two separate recessions.
   (c) Policy mistakes contributed to making the recession longer and more severe.
   (d) President Roosevelt promised balanced budgets during his first election campaign.

5. Which of the following is true?
   (a) Monetary policy was more helpful than fiscal policy during the Great Depression.
   (b) Taxes were raised on several occasions during the 1930s.
   (c) The Federal Reserve did not act to protect the gold standard in the 1930s, preferring to focus on the drop in bank lending as a priority.
   (d) The countries that abandoned the gold standard took a longer time period to begin economic recovery than countries that maintained the gold standard.

6. Which of the following is false?
   (a) There is often a tradeoff between a nation's exchange rate goals and its goals for income growth and employment.
   (b) Protecting a currency from depreciation may harm the domestic economy.
   (c) The desire to protect the exchange rate may conflict with the needs of the domestic economy.
   (d) Preventing a fall in the value of the domestic currency helps maintain jobs and growth.

7. An increase in government spending would cause
   (a) household incomes to decrease.
   (b) interest rates to fall.
   (c) the currency to appreciate.
   (d) national income to decrease.

8. Exchange rate
   (a) depreciation switches some consumer spending from domestic goods to foreign goods.
   (b) appreciation switches some consumer spending from foreign goods to domestic goods.
   (c) changes do not change the proportion of spending between domestic and foreign goods.
   (d) depreciation switches some consumer spending from foreign goods to domestic goods.

9. Which of the following is true?
   (a) Expansionary monetary policy has an even larger positive effect on national income than expansionary fiscal policy.
   (b) Contractionary monetary policy has a smaller negative effect on national income than contractionary fiscal policy.
   (c) Expansionary fiscal policy has a larger positive effect on national income than expansionary monetary policy.
   (d) Contractionary fiscal policy has a larger negative effect on national income than contractionary monetary policy.

10. Which of the following will increase imports the most?
    (a) expansionary monetary policy
    (b) expansionary fiscal policy
    (c) contractionary monetary policy
    (d) contractionary fiscal policy

11. Which of the following is an expenditure switching policy?
    (a) an increase in interest rates
    (b) a cut in government spending
    (c) a depreciation of the currency
    (d) a decrease in the money supply

12. Which of the following is an expenditure reducing policy?
    (a) an open market sale of securities that raises interest rates
    (b) an increase in government spending
    (c) an increase in taxes
    (d) an increase in the money supply

■ Answers to Vocabulary

1. expansionary monetary policy
2. intermediate inputs
3. contractionary fiscal policy
4. J-curve
5. multiplier effect
6. contractionary monetary policy
7. fiscal policy
8. aggregate demand (AD)
9. expenditure reducing policy
10. monetary policy
11. expansionary fiscal policy
12. open market operations
13. adjustment process
14. aggregate supply (AS)
15. expenditure switching policy

■ Answers to Chapter Review

1. They assume responsibility for keeping economic growth on track, unemployment low, and prices stable.

2. The income for the economy as a whole equals the value of its output.

3. On the horizontal portion, GDP is far below capacity and output can expand without raising prices. In the middle section, output can expand, but the price level rises as we get closer and closer to the economy's full production capacity. The vertical section represents a situation where no new output is possible for the time being or the full employment level of GDP.

4. Changes in consumer spending, business investment, government spending, taxes, or exports all shift aggregate demand.

5. as a shift to the right of the aggregate supply curve

6. A small change in initial spending works its way through the economy and creates a larger change in output as the spending stimulates production, which gives people more income, which stimulates further spending and production.

7. Imports rise as income and spending rise.

8. Fiscal policies rely on changes in government spending and taxes whereas monetary policies use changes in the money supply and interest rates to affect output, employment, and the price level.

9. Expansionary fiscal policy tends to cause inflation. It is difficult to accurately measure the size of the multiplier. It can cause different effects based on its financing. It is also politically cumbersome in terms of negotiating, enacting, and implementing the changes.

10. open market operations (buying and selling bonds)

11. Social Security, the Fair Labor Standards Act, the Securities and Exchange Commission, the Federal Deposit Insurance Corporation, the Tennessee Valley Authority, and many others

12. Fiscal policy was not helpful in that tax increases contributed to contractionary pressures. Monetary policy was a disaster, raising interest rates and decreasing the money supply.

13. Interest rate increases cause that nation's currency to appreciate and interest rate decreases cause a nation's currency to depreciate.

14. Because it leads to lower interest rates, expansionary monetary policy causes a nation's currency to depreciate.

15. a drop in national income and potentially recession

16. When income rises due to expansionary fiscal policy, interest rates rise as the demand for money increases. This causes the currency to depreciate. Contractionary fiscal policy would lead interest rates to fall and the currency to appreciate.

17. Monetary policy has a more robust effect on national income because it increases domestic expenditure and reduces imports as the currency depreciates. But fiscal policy has a more predictable impact on the current account because imports increase from the rise in income and also from the appreciation in the currency.

18. exchange rate changes and changes in domestic prices

19. turn domestic expenditures away from foreign-produced products toward domestic products (expenditure switching) and reduce the overall level of demand in the economy (expenditure reducing)

20. to avoid inflation
21. to avoid recession
22. There is a lags of many months before the exchange rate change begins to impact trade. The initial reaction is often an increase in the value of imports, making the current account deficit worse in the short run.
23. The 1980s saw large budget deficits and an appreciated U.S. dollar from both fiscal and monetary policy. The 1990s saw the budget deficit reduced and eventually in surplus, but sharp increases in investment spending occurred. A consumption boom was fueled partly by a drop in savings. Slow growth in trading partners characterized both periods, but in the 1990s, foreign capital poured into the United States, causing the dollar to appreciate.
24. No international organizations exist and none are possible without large decreases in national sovereignty; rarely do nations find it in their own interests to pursue the same policies as their trading partners because they enter and leave expansions and contractions at different points in time; and one policy doesn't suit all their situations.

■ Answers to Just the Facts

1. right; increasing; decreasing
2. increasing; decreasing; aggregate demand; left
3. buys; increase; lower
4. higher; less
5. 25; 26
6. 1929; 1933; 1937; 1938
7. inflow; appreciate
8. contractionary; monetary; recession
9. more
10. imports; diminishes
11. definite; indeterminate
12. current; deficits
13. 9.5; 7

■ Answers to Review Quiz

1. B
2. A
3. D
4. A
5. B
6. D

7. C
8. D
9. A
10. B
11. C
12. A

Chapter 12
International Financial Crises

■ Vocabulary

For each numbered description, write in the correct term from the list provided.

austerity
banking crisis
Basel Capital Accord
capital control
capital requirement
collective action clause
conditionality
contagion effect
crony capitalism
data dissemination standard
disintermediation
exchange rate crisis
financial crisis
information disclosure
intermediation
international financial architecture
lender of last resort
moral hazard
standstill
supervisory review
tranches

1. The IMF's standard for data reporting _____

2. Governments use state-owned banks or put pressure on private banks to make loans to firms in order to achieve specific economic development goals or to satisfy important political constituencies. These loans may not meet the market criteria for lending and are implicitly or explicitly backed by the government _____

3. The IMF officially recognizes the need for a country in crisis to temporarily stop interest and principal repayments on its debt _____

4. Requires each lender to agree to a collective mediation between all lenders and the debtor in the event of a crisis _____

5. IMF installments on the total loan, where each additional release of the loan funding depends on the completion of a set of reform targets _____

6. Reducing budget deficits by cutting government spending and increasing taxes, devaluing the currency, and perhaps temporarily limiting imports _____

7. The changes in economic policy that borrowing nations are required to make in order to receive IMF loans _____

8. Policy to limit the movement of capital _____

9. Bank must disclose all relevant information that lenders, investors and depositors need to understand the full scope of the bank's operations _____

10. A set of recommended best practices for international banking that emphasize capital requirements, supervisory review, and information disclosure _____

11. Reduce moral hazard by requiring the owners of the banking institution to invest a percentage of their own capital in their bank so that bank losses are personal losses to shareholders and bank owners as well as to the depositors _____

12. Oversight to assist with risk management and to provide standards for daily business practices _____

13. There is an incentive to withhold essential information or to act in a manner that creates personal benefits at the expense of the common goal _____

14. A banking system becomes unable to perform its normal lending functions, and some or all of a nation's banks are threatened with insolvency _____

15. An exchange rate crisis, a banking crisis or some combination of the two _____

16. Function banks perform between savers and borrowers when they pool the savings of households and make them available to businesses for investment _____

17. When banks cannot act as intermediaries between savers and investors, perhaps because the businesses they lent to have become insolvent and the bank is not able to pay back its depositors and it becomes insolvent as well _____

18. A sudden and unexpected collapse in the value of a nation's currency _____

19. When a financial crisis spreads from one country to another _____

20. The IMF and other multilateral institutions with a role in international financial relations _____

21. An institution that provides liquidity during a financial crisis to keep the crisis from getting worse or from damaging third parties not sharing the initial problems that sparked the crisis _____

■ Chapter Review

Answer the questions in the space provided below each.

1. What are the vulnerable points in an economy to a financial crisis?

2. Describe a banking crisis.

3. How does a banking crisis damage the wider economy?

4. Describe an exchange rate crisis.

5. What are the most common types of macroeconomic imbalances?

6. How did industrial development policies in developing countries affect government budget deficits?

7. How do deficits that are financed by borrowed money impact the exchange rate?

8. Why are crawling pegs problematic?

9. What is the policy prescription to deal with macroeconomic imbalances?

10. How can volatile capital flows lead to a crisis?

11. If a banking sector borrows internationally and lends locally, how can this intensify a crisis?

12. How can a crisis become a self-fulfilling prophecy?

13. Why are these types of problems troubling to economists and policymakers?

14. How can countries avoid crises caused by volatile financial flows?

15. What signs of macroeconomic imbalance existed in the Mexican peso crisis? What positive policies were in place?

16. What factors led to a reassessment of Mexico by portfolio managers in 1994?

17. What policies did Mexico use to respond to the crisis?

18. What lessons were learned from the peso crisis?

19. Describe the moral hazard problem with promises to bail out the financial system in the event of crisis.

20. What steps have been taken to reduce the moral hazard problem?

21. What are "hard" pegs and why do economists recommend them as opposed to crawling pegs?

22. What are the benefits and costs of capital mobility?

23. How are capital flows restricted?

24. What were some of the background factors that contributed to the East Asian financial crisis?

25. What three issues in crisis management remain unresolved regarding the Asian financial crisis?

26. What two issues are the center of the debate about reforming the international financial architecture?

27. Why is IMF conditionality controversial?

■ Just the Facts

1. Between 1990 and 1993 Mexico experienced capital inflows of about _____ billion per year, the most of any developing country.

2. In 1994, Mexico was saving about _____ percent of its GDP and having investment spending of more than _____ percent of GDP.

3. In December 1994 President Zedillo announced a _____ percent devaluation in the peso when currency traders were expecting a _____ percent devaluation, which sent markets into a turmoil.

4. By March 1995, the peso had fallen more than _____ percent against the U.S. dollar compared to its December 1994 value.

5. In the Asian financial crisis _____ restricted capital outflows even though experts warned it might undermine investor confidence, but still had a recovery similar to others that did not use such restrictions.

6. The East Asian financial crisis began in _____ during _____.

7. The outward symptoms of the financial crisis included _____, _____ and _____.

8. The most severely affected countries in the Asian financial crisis all had _____ that averaged _____ percent of GDP.

9. Except for Singapore and Taiwan, every country affected by the East Asian financial crisis had a _____ in 1998.

10. IMF loan rules regarding _____, _____ and _____ are the subject of great debate.

■ Review Quiz

Check your mastery of the chapter by selecting the letter that gives the correct answer to each question.

1. Which of the following is not a likely result of a banking crisis?
   (a) a decrease in investment spending
   (b) a decrease in consumption spending
   (c) an increase in national income as spending is diverted from imports to domestically produced products
   (d) an increase in the number of financial institution insolvencies

2. Which of the following is false?
   (a) An exchange rate crisis can happen under a fixed, flexible, or intermediate type of exchange rate system.
   (b) Under a fixed exchange rate system, an exchange rate crisis would involve the loss of international reserves.
   (c) Under a flexible exchange rate system, an exchange rate crisis involves a rapid depreciation of the currency.
   (d) Current research suggests that countries that use a pegged exchange rate are less vulnerable to exchange rate crises.

3. For both banking crises and exchange rate crises it is likely nations will experience
   (a) a steep recession.
   (b) a period of slower growth but no recession.
   (c) an expanding economy due to rising exports and falling imports.
   (d) an increase in investment spending.

4. Which of the following is not a symptom of a macroeconomic imbalance?
   (a) large government budget deficits
   (b) high growth rates for the money supply
   (c) an overvalued real exchange rate
   (d) a current account surplus

5. Devaluations
   (a) undermine faith in the government's ability to manage the economy.
   (b) never have political complications.
   (c) are helpful if they are relatively small.
   (d) help groups in the domestic economy that depend on foreign goods.

6. Austerity calls for
   (a) tax cuts.
   (b) government spending increases.
   (c) devaluation of the domestic currency.
   (d) subsidies to encourage imports.

7. Which of the following is true?
   (a) A banking sector that borrows locally and lends internationally will be hurt if its domestic currency devalues.
   (b) If banks obtain long term loans on the international market and lend in their domestic market only short term, they are very vulnerable to short run movements in international capital markets.
   (c) If bank assets are very liquid, they are vulnerable to short term movements in capital markets.
   (d) For banks that have long term assets that are illiquid, such as real estate loans, and short term international debt, they can have good assets and still be very vulnerable to volatile capital flows.

8. Which of the following is false?
   (a) Economists and policymakers are particularly troubled by the self-fulfilling type of crisis.
   (b) Depending on the response of international lenders, there are different possible outcomes to a crisis.
   (c) As long as international lenders are willing to extend credit while banks deal with their illiquid assets, a crisis can be avoided.
   (d) Banks that are fundamentally sound never face insolvency from an international crisis caused by volatile capital flows.

9. Which of the following is a lesson of the Mexican peso crisis?
   (a) Relying on large inflows of foreign savings to fund domestic investment is a sound strategy.
   (b) Pegged exchange rate systems are best for arranging an orderly devaluation of a currency.
   (c) Foreign portfolio investment combined with an overvalued currency can be problematic and add to the crisis as investors sell it off rapidly.
   (d) Economists believe fixed exchange rates combined with completely discretionary monetary policy are the best option to avoid crises.

10. Which of the following is true?
    (a) The problem of moral hazard is inescapable if there is a general policy of protecting the financial system from collapse.
    (b) Crony capitalism was not a contributing factor in the East Asian finanical crisis.
    (c) No action has been taken internationally to deal with the problems of weak financial sectors.
    (d) Capital mobility does not impose any costs in the international economy.

■ Answers to Vocabulary

1. data dissemination standard
2. crony capitalism
3. standstill
4. collective action clause

5. tranches
6. austerity
7. conditionality
8. capital control
9. information disclosure
10. Basel Capital Accord
11. capital requirement
12. supervisory review
13. moral hazard
14. banking crisis
15. financial crisis
16. intermediation
17. disintermediation
18. exchange rate crisis
19. contagion effect
20. international financial architecture
21. lender of last resort

■ Answers to Chapter Review

1. the exchange rate and the banking system
2. When banks become unable to intermediate loans, typically because the value of their assets (loans) declines sharply and their liabilities to depositors and others becomes greater than the value of their loans.
3. As depositors lose their savings, spending decreases and new investment stops by the lack of lending. Both cut spending and national income and output drop correspondingly.
4. a sudden and unexpected collapse in the value of a nation's currency that leads to a steep recession, perhaps through a banking crisis
5. large external debts combined with any sort of change in asset prices or expectations about future ability to pay; overly expansionary fiscal policies that create large government budget deficits financed by high rates of growth for the money supply; a large and growing current account deficit
6. Government budgets became the engine of investment spending as governments owned whole industries in addition to their normal roles. When this was combined with poor tax collection systems that made governments sell large numbers of bonds, they wound up having the central bank as a major purchaser of the government debt, rapidly expanding the money supply.
7. Inflation usually results and can lead the real exchange rate to be overvalued if nominal rates adjust too slowly. If people suspect the currency is overvalued, capital flight begins and forces a devaluation.

8. Devaluations are politically difficult because they undermine faith in the government's ability to manage the economy. Sudden devaluations hurt some groups (making them unpopular) but delay can cause a deeper crisis since a small change may no longer be sufficient to stem the outflow.

9. Austerity, meaning a combination of expenditure switching and expenditure reducing policies. This means reducing budget deficits by raising taxes and cutting spending to reduce demand while devaluing the currency to reduce imports and increase domestic production.

10. Technology has made it possible to move vast sums of financial capital from one market to the other in a short period of time and policies of openness to attract foreign capital have removed most barriers to doing so. This makes countries with appropriate fiscal and monetary policies vulnerable if underlying weaknesses in other countries spark a crisis. Portfolio managers look to each other for information and thus herd behavior turns trickles into floods that make even otherwise healthy financial sectors weak.

11. The borrowed funds have to be repaid with international currencies while the payments received come in the local currency. As the currency devalues, the borrowed sums increase while the value of the loans making payments decreases, potentially leading to insolvency, especially if the local loans are long term and illiquid and the international borrowing is short term.

12. If international lenders worry about solvency and stop making loans, the borrowers become insolvent as they all seek to simultaneously sell assets in the short run at falling prices.

13. There are multiple possible outcomes. Only one is a crisis and the crisis is caused by unnecessary behavior on the part of lenders and borrowers and could be avoided. The banks are illiquid not insolvent and the crisis is not pre-determined or necessary.

14. Banks need to watch the maturity match of their debts and assets. This may require more bank supervision and regulation. International lenders need better information about the activities of their borrowers. This requires standard accounting, transparency and greater information flows. Agencies such as the IMF need to better distinguish insolvency and illiquidity in their emergency lending.

15. Macroeconomic imbalances included an overvalued real exchange rate and a large current account deficit. On the positive side, the Mexican government operated a relatively austere fiscal policy, inflation was down, and Mexico was experiencing large capital inflows.

16. Global capital markets were more conservative and risk averse. There was a revolt in Chiapas, Mexico against the federal government. A leading presidential candidate was assassinated. This lead investors to reassess whether Mexico was the safe, stable and modernizing economy they thought, and to begin reducing their peso-denominated assets.

17. In the short run, loans and lines of credit were established with the IMF and the United States. Austerity measures included cuts in government spending, increased taxes, and reduced consumption.

18. For Mexico, relying too heavily on large foreign inflows to finance investment was unstable. Too much was in short term portfolios rather than long term direct investment. Pegged exchange rate systems make it difficult to arrange an orderly devaluation as any single change may not be large enough and may cause the government to lose credibility. Economists think flexible exchange rates or completely fixed exchange rates with no discretionary monetary policy are better.

19. If the costs of failure are removed, the incentive for decision makers inside financial institutions to make responsible decisions and to take normal precautions are also removed. Governments can't afford to let their financial systems go under but can't let their financial sectors expect bailouts.

20. The Basel Capital Accord has been adopted by more than 100 countries. It sets capital requirements, requirements for supervisory review and for information disclosure.

21. A hard peg is basically a fixed exchange rate system and could include dollarization and the use of currency boards. Credibility of the peg is most important to its survival and crawling pegs have had credibility problems, especially when the real exchange rate becomes overvalued.

22. The benefits include that investors can put financial capital where it earns the highest return, which raises welfare by putting capital in its most valuable use. Capital inflows allow nations to invest more than they would by relying on their own savings. The cost is potential macroeconomic crisis from volatile capital flows.

23. Usually by limiting transactions that are part of the financial account of the balance of payments.

24. Investors were seeking higher growth and government policies were thought to be very stable and favorable for growth in this region so there were tremendous capital inflows. Most currencies were pegged to the U.S. dollar and the dollar was appreciating internationally, causing the real exchange rates to be overvalued. Export earnings were damaged by the currency values. These revealed other weaknesses in corporate structures, regulatory systems, and the financial sector, especially in the area of transparency.

25. Was the IMF wrong to advise borrowing countries to raise interest rates to defend their currencies? Were there moral hazard problems? Are capital controls helpful as a temporary measure to stem a crisis?

26. the role of an international lender of last resort and the type of conditions this lender might place on borrowing nations

27. overrides national sovereignty and imposes contractionary macroeconomic policies

■ Answers to Just the Facts

1. $23 billion
2. 14; 20
3. 15; 20–30
4. 50
5. Malaysia
6. Thailand; July 1997
7. steep depreciations; capital flight; financial and industrial sector bankruptcies
8. large trade deficits; 5.2
9. recession
10. interest rate; payback period; size of loan

■ Answers to Review Quiz

1. C
2. D
3. A
4. D
5. A

6. C
7. D
8. D
9. C
10. A

Chapter 13
Economic Integration in North America

■ Vocabulary

For each numbered description, write in the correct term from the list provided.

Auto Pact
Brady Plan
Canada-U.S. Trade Agreement (CUSTA)
debt crisis
demand-pull factors
Enterprise of the Americas Initiative (EAI)
export processing zone (EPZ)
Free Trade Agreement of the Americas (FTAA)
import substitution industrialization (ISI)
Lost Decade
maquiladora
North American Development Bank (NADBank)
North American Free Trade Agreement (NAFTA)
North American Agreement on Environmental Cooperation
North American Agreement on Labor Cooperation
purchasing power parity
social networks
supply-push factors

1. Purpose was to ensure that capital continued to flow to Latin America, to provide relief from the debt crisis of the 1980s, to liberalize trade, and to create incentive for Latin American countries to continue with political and economic reform _____

2. Treaty being negotiated by nations from the Western Hemisphere, originally intended as a significant market opening but likely to result in a series of non-binding agreements _____

3. Forces inside Mexico that are pushing people to leave to seek work in the United States
   _____

4. Newcomers have contacts or family on who they can rely while they are establishing themselves
   _____

5. Labor shortages or strong demand for labor in the United States leads foreign workers to migrate
   _____

6. Side agreement requiring national enforcement of environmental laws and creating an institutional framework for the discussion and resolution of transboundary environmental problems
   _____

7. Helps finance environmental clean up at the border _____

8. Side agreement on labor issues requires both the United States and Mexico to enforce their labor laws, especially laws related to child labor, minimum wages and workplace safety, and to permit investigators to examine infringements and if necessary impose fines _____

9. U.S. plan for debt relief that led to Mexico getting a reduction in its debt of about 10 percent and to a change in international perceptions about the country and its prospects _____

10. Agreement that removed trade barriers for autos and auto parts between Canada and the United States _____

11. Development strategy that favors an inward orientation and self-sufficiency over trade and domestic production over imported products _____

12. Firms located in the export processing zone in Mexico _____

13. Agreement that created a free trade area for Canada and the United States _____

14. The 1980s when almost no GDP growth occurred in Mexico and Latin America generally _____

15. Area where foreign firms were encouraged to set up assembly-type operation and escape Mexican tariffs on imported parts and materials as long as the assembled products were exported _____

16. Makes adjustments for differences in prices between nations using an artificial exchange rate _____

17. Free trade agreement between the United States, Canada, and Mexico _____

18. A country lacks the foreign exchange rate reserves to make interest and principle payments on its international borrowing _____

■ Chapter Review

Answer the questions in the space provided below each.

1. What are the potential problems with comparing national incomes across the NAFTA countries? How are these measurement problems addressed?
   _____

2. Why might trade agreements between the United States and Mexico be more controversial than trade agreements between the United States and Canada?
   _____

3. How did free trade agreements between the United States and Canada get started?
   _____

4. What two trends was Canada trying to address in negotiating CUSTA?
   _____

5. Was CUSTA the subject of great debate?

6. What exceptions were granted for Canadian industries within the CUSTA agreement?

7. What economic policies had Mexico followed since the end of World War II until the 1980s?

8. Supporters of ISI emphasized a three stage strategy. Describe the stages.

9. Describe the success and failure of ISI policies prior to the 1980s.

10. What happened in the 1980s that triggered a shift away from ISI policies?

11. What happened in 1981 to Mexico's economy?

12. How did U.S. monetary policy impact the debt situation of Mexico?

13. Why are the 1980s known as the Lost Decade? What was happening to economic variables during that time?

14. What were the three main lessons from the debt crisis of 1982?

15. What did President Salinas perceive as his key tasks for fixing problems with the Mexican economy?

16. What was Mexico seeking from NAFTA?

17. Describe the three generations of maquiladora plants.

18. Describe three important features of NAFTA.

19. Which issues were especially debated in the United States regarding NAFTA and which groups were especially opposed?

20. What are the three factors that determine the number of migrants from Mexico to the United States?

21. What are unintended consequences of U.S. anti-immigration enforcement efforts?

22. What has NAFTA meant for Mexico?

23. Why is NAFTA significant for U.S.-Mexican relations and U.S.-Latin American relations more generally?

24. What are the prospects for the Free Trade Agreement of the Americas?

■ Just the Facts

1. In 2002, the NAFTA market contained _____ million residents, _____ total GNP and GNP per capita of _____.

2. NAFTA went into effect on _____.

3. Using table 13.1, in 2002 purchasing power parity terms, Mexican GNP per person is _____, but if the pesos were converted to U.S. dollars to be spent in the United States, it would only buy _____ worth of goods and services.

4. According to the chapter, Canada's index of openness for 2002 was _____ percent, Mexico's was _____ percent, and the United States' was _____ percent. By this measure, trade was most important for the economy of _____.

5. _____ and _____ trade more than any other two countries in the world.

6. From 1989 to 2002, U.S. exports to Canada increased _____ percent and imports from Canada increased _____ percent.

7. The Canada-United States Trade Agreement (CUSTA) was implemented _____, or exactly _____ years before NAFTA.

8. Free trade agreements between the United States and Canada started with the _____ industry in the year _____.

9. In Mexico, _____ is a government owned company that has a monopoly on oil exploration, development, and sales.

10. In 1982, the deficit of the federal government of Mexico reached _____ percent of GDP.

11. Between 1983 and 1988 in Mexico, real wages (rose, fell) by _____ percent. Between 1982 and 1986, Mexico's inflation adjusted GDP (rose, fell) by _____ percent.

12. Between 1990 and 1993, Mexico attracted _____ billion in outside capital or about _____ dollars that went to developing countries from private sources.

13. Approximately _____ percent of U.S.-Mexican trade is intrafirm.

14. A firm located in the export processing zone in Mexico is called a _____, and by 2003 these firms employed more than _____ workers and were responsible for _____ of total Mexican exports.

15. Mexico's largest source of U.S. dollars is its (oil industry, maquiladoras, residents working abroad, tourism industry).

16. In 2002, total compensation costs averaged _____ in Mexico per production worker versus _____ in the United States.

17. About _____ percent of the maquiladora industry is located in the the Mexican states adjacent to the U.S. border and employment in these firms is (more, less, similarly) synchronized with the business cycle in the United States than would be the case in the rest of Mexico.

18. A (demand-pull, supply-push, social network) factor that is increasing the number of Mexican migrants to the United States are Mexican policy changes in agriculture that are designed to reduce the percent of its labor force engaged in agriculture from _____ percent to _____ percent by the end of this decade.

19. Mexico's economy is less than _____ percent as large as the United States' economy.

■ Review Quiz

Check your mastery of the chapter by selecting the letter that gives the correct answer to each question.

1. Which of the following is false?
    (a) The NAFTA market is very rich.
    (b) NAFTA combines nations at very different levels of economic development.
    (c) The gap between per capita incomes in the United States and Mexico adds social and political tensions to NAFTA that did not exist for CUSTA.
    (d) Mexico accounts for a large portion of Canada's trade.

2. When comparing small market countries with large market countries,
    (a) small markets are less dependent on trade than large markets.
    (b) small markets are more able to realize economies of scale.
    (c) small markets can produce a greater variety of output.
    (d) trade allows small market countries to overcome limitations caused by market size.

3. Which of the following is false?
    (a) As measured by the index of openness, trade is more important to Canada than to Mexico.
    (b) Canada and Mexico are both more dependent of trade than the United States.
    (c) GNP per capita is higher in Canada than in the United States.
    (d) The United States trades more with Canada than it does with Mexico.

4. Which of the following is false?
   (a) Since the signing of CUSTA, U.S.-Canadian trade has more than doubled.
   (b) Initially when CUSTA was signed, U.S.-Canadian trade grew, but then there was a period of declining trade.
   (c) In 2002, U.S. trade with Canada was worth $370 billion.
   (d) CUSTA was not the first trade agreement between Canada and the United States.

5. At the time CUSTA was negotiated,
   (a) the trade agreement was very controversial in the United States.
   (b) Canadians feared the loss of jobs to more competitive U.S. industries.
   (c) U.S. media companies were highly successful at getting freer access to the Canadian market.
   (d) the Canadian federal and state governments had huge budget problems that entailed cuts in social program spending because of trade.

6. Which of the following is true? Between 1950 and 1973, ISI policies in Mexico
   (a) were successful in shifting Mexico toward greater industrial production.
   (b) reduced the tendencies toward corruption in the Mexican economy.
   (c) led to slower GDP per capita growth rates in purchasing power parity terms than were experienced by Canada and the United States, but higher growth in nominal terms.
   (d) helped Mexico's export sector become more competitive.

7. The maquiladora industry
   (a) has not been as important for Mexican employment as prior guest worker programs such as the bracero program.
   (b) makes Mexican firms less dependent on the U.S. business cycle for their production and sales.
   (c) has become a more important source of U.S. dollars for Mexico than the oil industry.
   (d) is mostly located in central and southern Mexico.

8. Which of the following is false? NAFTA
   (a) reduced trade barriers on most goods and services for the participating countries.
   (b) allowed U.S. firms to move operations to Mexico, which hadn't been possible before.
   (c) specified North American content requirements for products in order to be eligible for free trade.
   (d) created a dispute resolution process.

9. Which of the following is false?
   (a) In the U.S. internal debate about NAFTA, the focus has been its effect on jobs.
   (b) Economists believe free trade creates increased production efficiency by reallocating resources.
   (c) Dislocated workers mean that free trade agreements aren't working to help the domestic economy.
   (d) It is unlikely that expanded trade with Mexico will have a large impact on the U.S. economy.

10. Demand-pull factors in illegal immigration would include
    (a) friends and relatives already living in the United States.
    (b) recession and poor economic conditions in Mexico.
    (c) changes in Mexican agricultural policy that push people off the farm.
    (d) high demand for agricultural labor in the United States.

■ Answers to Vocabulary

1. Brady Plan
2. Free Trade Agreement of the Americas (FTAA)
3. supply-push factors
4. social networks
5. demand-pull factors
6. North American Agreement on Environmental Cooperation
7. North American Development Bank (NADBank)
8. North American Agreement on Labor Cooperation
9. Enterprise of the Americas Initiative (EAI)
10. Auto Pact
11. import substitution industrialization (ISI)
12. maquiladora
13. Canada-U.S. Trade Agreement (CUSTA)
14. Lost Decade
15. export processing zone (EPZ)
16. purchasing power parity
17. North American Free Trade Agreement (NAFTA)
18. debt crisis

■ Answers to Chapter Review

1. Fluctuations in the exchange rate can lead to different values without reflecting actual changes in output. Real prices can vary across the countries for non-tradeable goods. Purchasing power parity comparisons are a more accurate way of comparing incomes and are calculated using an artificial exchange rate to correct for price differences.

2. The difference in the level of economic development between the United States and Mexico is greater so political and social tensions are larger. These issues include issues related to immigration and labor and environmental standards.

3. The Auto Pact of 1965 created a single, combined market for automobiles, and autos and auto parts remain the single largest component of trade between the two nations.

4. The United States was expanding its use of trade barriers and protectionist practices. Canadian industry needed to restructure to become more internationally competitive.

5. In the United States, it was not greatly debated. In Canada, it was hotly debated with Canadians fearing competition from U.S. firms, the loss of social programs, and the domination of Canadian culture by U.S. media and entertainment.

6. Canada is allowed to impose quantitative restrictions on imports of "cultural" products, including imposing domestic content requirements for television, radio and theater.

7. Import substitution industrialization (ISI), which emphasized self sufficiency over trade and the substitution of domestic manufacturing industries for imports.

8. First, the nation begins producing simple consumer nondurable products, then it would shift to more complex consumer goods and intermediate industrial goods. Finally, the nation would be able to produce more complex industrial goods.

9. From 1950 to 1973, Mexico had higher growth than the United States and Canada and had favorable growth compared to other regions and production shifted in Mexico toward greater industrial production. Problems included a lack of flexibility to produce exports and the creation of conditions that fostered corruption.

10. a severe international debt crisis

11. World oil prices began to fall, which decreased Mexico's income both at the time and for the future, which hurt its ability to service its large international debt and damaged its credit worthiness.

12. Most of Mexico's debt was to commercial banks at variable interest rates. U.S. monetary policy aimed at fighting inflation raised interest rates to extraordinarily high levels, which raised the cost of servicing Mexico's debt at the same time its oil revenues were falling.

13. Mexican (and Latin American) GDP growth was nearly nonexistent during that time. Foreign capital stopped flowing, credit was scarce, investment declined, the government budget was cut, the peso devalued, all of which contributed to a severe recession. Inflation also resulted as imported goods became more expensive. The real incomes of the middle class fell sharply.

14. Mexico had to change its management of its macroeconomy. The Mexican government could no longer use public spending as an engine for economic growth. Markets needed a larger role to attract the capital needed for investment and growth.

15. reduce the costs of servicing Mexico's international debt, create a climate in which Mexicans would be willing to bring home the financial capital they had sent abroad, and to attract foreign investment

16. to tie up the economic reforms Mexico had made in an international agreement to increase Mexican credibility, access to the United States market through Mexico to increase foreign investment

17. First plants were labor-intensive assembly operations that used unskilled, low-wage workers and very limited technology. Second generation plants used automated and semi-automated processes and a higher proportion of technicians and engineers. The third generation plants use advanced production techniques, perform research and development, and operate at the technological frontier.

18. most forms of trade barriers were removed, North American content requirements were set for free trade, a dispute resolution process was put in place

19. Blue-collar industrial labor unions were the most vocal opponents over fears about job security and differences in labor standards between the United States and Mexico. There were concerns about differences in environmental standards and especially about pollution on the U.S.-Mexican border where populations are growing. Illegal immigration is a highly contentious issue in U.S.-Mexican relations and some proponents of NAFTA argued that it would reduce migration.

20. Demand-pull factors are the attraction of U.S. jobs. Supply-push factors are the conditions in Mexico that make people want to leave. Social networks attract migrants to communities where family and friends are already established.

21. More migrants are dying as they try to cross in more extreme areas; migrants are staying longer in the United States as it becomes more difficult to cross back and forth.

22. It has solidified its openness and served as an impetus for a broad set of reforms in trade, agriculture, industrial policy, and the legal system.

23. Mexico is the most populous Spanish speaking country, has the second largest Latin American GDP, and has been at the forefront of economic reform toward openness and market orientation. It has signed the most free trade agreements of any nation in the world. In the past, U.S. aggression and Mexican nationalism has made cooperation and collaboration difficult. New institutions, especially at the regional level of the U.S.-Mexican border make more cooperation possible.

24. A set of nonbinding agreements will take effect, but formal binding commitments at the present are unlikely given the current situation in Brazil and the United States.

■ Answers to Just the Facts

1. 420; $11.4 trillion; $27,115
2. January 1, 1994
3. $8,540; $5,913
4. 87; 65; 26; Canada
5. Canada; the United States
6. 105; 147
7. January 1, 1989; 5
8. auto; 1965
9. Pemex or Petroleos Mexicano
10. 14.1
11. fell; 40 to 50; fell; 15
12. $90; one in every five
13. 25 to 35
14. maquila; one million; one half
15. maquiladoras
16. $2.38; $21.33
17. 80; more
18. supply-push; 26; 16
19. 5

■ Answers to Review Quiz

1. D
2. D
3. C
4. B
5. B

6. A
7. C
8. B
9. C
10. D

Chapter 14
The European Union: Many Markets into One

■ Vocabulary

For each numbered description, write in the correct term from the list provided.

acquis communautaire
Common Agricultural Policy (CAP)
competitive devaluation
convergence criteria
Council of the European Union
Court of Auditors
Court of Justice
Delors Report
democratic deficit
euro
European Atomic Energy Community (EAEC or Euratom)
European Coal and Steel Community (ECSC)
European Commission
European Community (EC)
European currency unit (ecu)
European Economic Community (EEC)
European Monetary System (EMS)
European Parliament
European Union (EU)
exchange rate mechanism (ERM)
Maastricht Treaty
qualified majority
Single European Act (SEA)
subsidiarity
Treaty of Rome
Treaty on European Union

1. The world's most extensive set of farm price supports and farm income maintenance programs, which takes more than 50 percent of the EU budget each year _____

2. EU-wide rules that all prospective members must adopt that cover technical standards, environmental and technical inspections, banking supervision, public accounts, statistical requirements, and other elements of EU law _____

3. The primary legislative branch of the European Union, where each country has a set number of representatives based on population, and those representatives are ministers from each nation, with membership varying based on the topic under discussion _____

4. EU agreement that among other items set the steps necessary to create a monetary union under a single currency _____

5. Objective measures set by the European Union to judge whether countries had brought their monetary and fiscal policies into harmony enough to participate in the common currency _____

6. Detailed 300 specific changes necessary to bring the European Union from a quasi-customs union to an economic union and laid out a time table for completing the changes _____

7. The executive body of the European Union _____

8. Law based on the Delor's report recommendations that amended the Treaty of Rome and established the European Union as a common market _____

9. A country devalues its currency in order to capture the export markets of another country _____

10. 1979 system designed to prevent extreme fluctuations in the European currency markets and to pave the way for monetary union _____

11. Each participating currency was tied to a weighted average of the other participating European currencies, but there was an exchange rate band allowing each to fluctuate several percentage points up or down from the fixed target _____

12. Establishes the relationship between national and EU areas of authority and between national and EU institutions _____

13. The average of the European currencies' values under the EMS, which was used as a unit of account but not for transactions _____

14. Legislative body with less power whose members are directly elected by the people for five-year terms and apportioned among the member states according to population _____

15. As the European nations expanded their agreements from economic issues to broader social and political ones, they changed their name to this _____

16. The lack of legislative clout for the popularly elected legislative body raised concern about EU governance and its responsiveness to the people _____

17. A majority of countries and 238 of 329 votes (72.3) _____

18. A political and economic integration of 25 member nations, with its own revenue and budget, a set of institutions for making laws and regulating areas of common interest, a common currency, and freedom of movement for people, money, goods, and services _____

19. Treaty signed in 1992 that led directly to the creation of common currency in 1999 _____

20. The common currency used in the European Union _____

21. The first step in the evolution of the European Union was this agreement to pool the coal and steel industries _____

22. Treaty signed in 1957 with the goal of creating a federation with a single, integrated market for goods, services, labor and capital that remains the fundamental agreement between EU members _____

23. Sought to jointly develop nuclear energy for peaceful purposes _____

24. Acts as the European Union's supreme court with responsibility for interpreting laws and treaties
    _____

25. Monitors the finances of the institutions and reports on the use and misuse of funds
    _____

26. The name used by the countries that signed the Treaty of Rome early in their integration
    _____

■ Chapter Review

Answer the questions in the space provided below each.

1. What are the three main treaties that form the European Union?

2. Which treaty forms the political and institutional structure of the European Union?

3. Which treaty created a free trade area for the participating countries?

4. Which treaty brought the participating countries to the common market level of integration?

5. Which treaty brought the participating countries to the economic union level of integration?

6. Do all nations participate in all the levels of integration? Describe any exceptions.

7. Describe the vision the founders had for the political structure of the European Union.

8. What areas of authority are under the control of the European Union? Which areas continue to be controversial?

9. What are the five main institutions of the European Union?

10. Which institution serves as the executive body of the European Union?

11. Which institution serves as the primary legislative branch of the European Union? Who makes up its members and how are votes determined?

12. Which institution of the European Union features direct election of representatives by the people? What responsibilities does it have?

13. Which institution serves as the supreme court? How are its decisions intrepreted by the national courts?

14. Describe the difference between widening and deepening of the European Union.

15. What was the European Monetary System and its exchange rate mechanism? How effective was it?

16. What caused the near collapse of the exchange rate mechanism in 1992?

17. What were the three choices nations exercised in reaction to the 1992 crisis?

18. What is the Schengen agreement? How does it relate to the European Union? Do all EU countries participate?

19. What are the "four freedoms?"

20. What were the gains from the Single European Act?

21. What were the major obstacles to implementing the Single European Act?

22. What explanations are given for why the Maastricht treaty was signed prior to the implementation of the Single European Act?

23. What are the benefits and costs of adopting a single currency?

24. What conditions would make a single currency optimal?

25. Why was a single currency implemented in the European Union when it seems that it did not meet the criteria for an optimal currency area?

26. What are some of the challenges in widening the European Union eastward?

Chapter 14 The European Union: Many Markets into One

■ Just the Facts

1. There are currently _____ members of the European Union, _____ of which use the euro as their official currency.

2. The total 2004 population of the European Union is _____ million and total GNP is _____ trillion.

3. The largest country and the most important economy in the European Union is _____.

4. The (NAFTA, EU) market has the larger population and the (NAFTA, EU) market has the larger total GNP.

5. The Treaty of Rome entered into force on _____ with _____ member nations participating.

6. The first agreements reached in the European community were for the _____ and _____ industries.

7. At the European Commission, votes are based on (population, economic strength, one vote per nation).

8. Currently there are _____ votes at the Council of the European Union and for issues that do not require unanimity, a qualified majority of _____ percent is required.

9. The presidency of the European Council rotates every _____ and gives each nation a chance to bring up its own legislative agenda.

10. The president of the European Union is elected by _____.

11. The total 2003 budget for the European Union was _____ billion euros, with _____ percent coming from the EU share of tariff revenue, _____ coming from a value-added tax levied on all countries, and _____ from the participating national governments.

12. The total budget of the European Union represents about _____ percent of total income in its region, while the total budget of the U.S. federal government is about _____ percent of total U.S. income.

13. The _____ Report was the basis for the (Treaty of Rome, Single European Act, Treaty on Economic Union, European Monetary System).

14. The European Union became a common market on _____.

15. Compared with the Single European Act, the Maastricht Treaty was (more, less) popular and (more, less) controversial.

16. Compared to Americans, Europeans are (more, less) mobile, which makes the EU region (more, less) likely to be an optimal currency area.

17. Agriculture took _____ percent of the EU budget in 2003.

■ Review Quiz

Check your mastery of the chapter by selecting the letter that gives the correct answer to each question.

1. Which of the following nations is not a member of the European Union but does participate in the four freedoms?
   (a) Spain
   (b) Norway
   (c) Greece
   (d) Portugal

2. Which of the following nations is a member of the European Union but does not participate in the common currency?
   (a) Switzerland
   (b) Norway
   (c) Finland
   (d) Sweden

3. Which of the following nations joined the European Union in 2004?
   (a) Malta
   (b) Greece
   (c) Romania
   (d) Iceland

4. Which agreement created a common market in the European Union?
   (a) Delors Report
   (b) Treaty on European Union
   (c) Single European Act
   (d) Schengen Agreement

5. Which of the following is true?
   (a) All nations that use the euro as their official currency are members of the European Union.
   (b) All nations that belong to the European Union use the euro as their official currency.
   (c) All nations that belong to the European Union fully participate in the Schengen Agreement.
   (d) All nations that participate in the Schengen Agreement are part of the European Union.

6. The Maastricht treaty
   (a) created a common market in the European Union.
   (b) outlined the four freedoms and gave nations the chance to choose the freedoms in which they would participate.
   (c) set the conditions and time line for the adoption of a common currency.
   (d) has been ratified by all members of the European Union.

7. Which of the following serves as the executive branch of the European Union?
   (a) the Court of Justice
   (b) the Council of the European Union
   (c) the European Parliament
   (d) The European Commission

8. Which of the following institutions has representatives that are popularly elected?
   (a) the Court of Auditors
   (b) the Council of the European Union
   (c) the European Parliament
   (d) The European Commission

9. Labor ministers from the various EU nations might meet and vote as part of the
   (a) the Court of Auditors.
   (b) the Council of the European Union.
   (c) the European Parliament.
   (d) The European Commission.

10. Which of the following is false?
    (a) The countries that ultimately adopted the euro were all nations that successfully met the criteria established under the Maastricht treaty.
    (b) Implementing a single currency in the European Union was much less popular and more controversial than creating a common market.
    (c) The benefits of adopting a common currency were uncertain and the costs were more certain.
    (d) Efforts to fix exchange rates in the Europe Union were not highly successful and the bands and targets had to be changed or in some cases abandoned by individual nations at various points in time.

11. Harmonizing technical standards was an important step in implementing
    (a) the Treaty of Rome.
    (b) Treaty on European Union.
    (c) Single European Act.
    (d) Schengen Agreement.

12. The Common Agricultural Policy
    (a) has not been very expensive for the European Union since most nations are industrialized.
    (b) does not distort agricultural markets.
    (c) takes the majority of the EU budget.
    (d) was relatively simple to extend to the 10 new EU members that joined in 2004.

■ Answers to Vocabulary

1. Common Agricultural Policy (CAP)
2. acquis communautaire
3. Council of the European Union
4. Maastricht Treaty
5. convergence criteria
6. Delors Report
7. Single European Act (SEA)
8. European Commission

9. competitive devaluation
10. European Monetary System (EMS)
11. exchange rate mechanism (ERM)
12. subsidiarity
13. European currency unit (ecu)
14. European Parliament
15. European Community (EC)
16. democratic deficit
17. qualified majority
18. European Union (EU)
19. Treaty on European Union
20. euro
21. European Coal and Steel Community (ECSC)
22. Treaty of Rome
23. European Atomic Energy Community (EAEC or Euratom)
24. Court of Justice
25. Court of Auditors
26. European Economic Community (EEC)

■ Answers to Chapter Review

1. the Treaty of Rome, the Single European Act, the Treaty on European Union
2. the Treaty of Rome
3. the Treaty of Rome
4. the Single European Act
5. the Treaty on European Union
6. There are nations that participate in the four freedoms (common market) but that don't participate in the European Union, such as Norway. Three nations participate in the European Union but don't participate in the euro—Denmark, Sweden, and the United Kingdom. None of the countries that joined the European Union in May 2004 currently use the euro, although they are all supposed to qualify to do so some day.
7. They envisioned a federation in which local, regional, national, and European authorities cooperate and complement one another, similar to the divisions of authority between local, regional/state, and national governments in the United States and Canada.
8. Environmental and regional policy, research and technological development and economic and monetary union; labor market policies, social policies and competition policies remain areas of controversy about the right policies and authority for setting those policies.
9. European Commission, Council of the European Union, European Parliament, the Court of Justice, and the Court of Auditors

10. European Commission

11. The Council of the European Union; ministers from the EU nations rotate depending on the issue to be decided; from 3 to 29 votes per nation depending on size with most issues requiring either unanimity or a 72.3 majority.

12. the European Parliament; veto powers over new membership, ability to amend some legislation, change parts of budget, question the Council and the Commission

13. the Court of Justice, its decisions are binding and take precedence over national court decisions for areas of EU authority

14. Widening involves extending the boundaries of the European Union to include new members while deepening involves economic and noneconomic activities that have the effect of increasing integration of the national economies.

15. It was designed to prevent extreme currency fluctuations by tying each participating nations' currency to a weighted average of the others. Each currency was allowed to fluctuate several percentage points above and below its fixed value to the weighted average. It was not very effective in the face of strong and determined market movement, but in general it lasted almost two decades with adjustments to the bands.

16. the reunification of Germany lead to higher interest rates in Germany to prevent inflation which lead other EU currencies to depreciate against the mark

17. Abandon the ERM (UK and Italy), stay within it and suffer recession domestically (France), devalue the center of the band and widen it (Spain)

18. It eliminates all passport and custom controls at the common borders of the participating nations and was formally incorporated into EU law in 1999. Some non-EU countries participate (Iceland, Norway), and some nations that formally participate (UK, Ireland) have not eliminated the border controls over fears over terrorism. The ability of the 10 latest EU members to enforce border controls at the perimeter will determine their future participation in the agreement.

19. freedom of movement for goods, services, capital, and labor

20. Increases in economic efficiency from reduced transport costs/distribution costs at the border, greater economies of scale, more competition

21. Concerns over the effects of restructuring, harmonizing technical standards, dealing with value-added taxes, and policies regarding public procurement

22. it completed actions not addressed in the Delors Report by the Single European Act, the pace of German unification perhaps created fears about Germany losing its focus on western Europe as it looked east, it was politically necessary given the changes of the Single European Act.

23. Benefits include reduced transactions costs and uncertainty over exchange rates. The costs are that nations can no longer pursue independent monetary policies.

24. if the participating nations have synchronized business cycles and mobile labor forces

25. Floating rates were politically undesirable, and the freedom of capital flows under the single European Act coupled with the inability of EU nations to maintain fixed exchange rates made adopting a single currency the best option.

26. Agriculture and agricultural policies and potential migration; rules of governance; difference in income between the old EU members and the new members; relationships between new EU members and nations farther to the east

■ Answers to Just the Facts

1. 25; 12 (as of 2004)
2. 453.7; $8.4
3. Germany
4. EU; NAFTA
5. January 1, 1958; six
6. coal; steel
7. one vote per nation
8. 329; 72.3
9. six months
10. the European Commission
11. 101.6; 14; 35; 50
12. 1.5; 20
13. Delors; Single European Act
14. January 1, 1993
15. less; more
16. less; less
17. 54

■ Answers to Review Quiz

1. B
2. D
3. A
4. C
5. A
6. C
7. D
8. C
9. B
10. A
11. C
12. C

Chapter 15
Trade and Policy Reform in Latin America

■ Vocabulary

For each numbered description, write in the correct term from the list provided.

Baker Plan
Brady Plan
Economic Commission on Latin America (ECLA, or CEPAL in Spanish)
economic populism
export pessimism
heterodox stabilization policy
import substitution industrialization (ISI)
Lost Decade
market failure
neoliberalism
orthodox stabilization policy
populism
structural reform policies
terms of trade (TOT)
Washington Consensus

1. The set of economic policy reforms that included governments implementing stabilization plans to get budget deficits and inflation under control, privatizing the government-owned parts of their economies, and opening trade policies, all of which emphasize less government involvement in the economy and more free market allocation of resources _____

2. A set of economic policies that constitute a broad consensus among both conservative and liberal economists _____

3. Minimizes government involvement in the economy and prescribes government spending cuts, tax reform, and control over money supply growth to fight inflation _____

4. Policies that focus on microeconomic level reforms such as the privatization of government-owned enterprises, deregulation, and trade policy reform _____

5. 1985 plan that tried to re-start capital flows to Latin America by renewing bank lending programs _____

6. Calls for government spending cuts, tax reform, control over money supply growth, and also wage and price freezes to fight inflation and to reduce inflationary expectations _____

7. Period of time following the debt crisis in Latin America that was marked by recession, inflation, and lack of investment _____

8. 1989 plan that called for creditors to restructure some of their Latin American debt into longer-term loans on better terms and to make some new loans, for multilateral agencies to make new loans at below market terms, and for borrowers to provide evidence of their commitment to economic reform in order to receive any new loans _____

9. Political style that is nationalist and that focuses on economic growth and income redistribution
   _____

10. Using expansionary fiscal and monetary policy to stimulate the economy without the usual constraints of worrying about inflation risks, budget deficits, and foreign exchange movements
    _____

11. The presence of externalities, market power, or other problems that lead the free market to misallocate resources and not obtain optimal outcomes for an economy _____

12. Industrial development policy that emphasized replacing imported manufactured goods with domestically produced ones through deliberate government policies such as subsidies, restrictions on foreign investment, and trade barriers _____

13. A United Nations agency headed for years by Raul Prebisch that pushed the ISI model of industrialization _____

14. The ratio of average export prices to average import prices _____

15. Prebisch's prediction that the terms of trade for the Latin American region would decline since it exported raw materials and imported finished goods _____

■ Chapter Review

Answer the questions in the space provided below each.

1. What are the common themes shared by all Latin American countries?

2. Describe economic growth in Latin America in the 20th century.

3. How were Latin American economies organized from the mid 19th century to the mid 20th century?

4. How were Latin American nations affected by World War I, the Depression, and World War II?

5. Why did Raul Prebisch predict that the terms of trade would decline for Latin America if they continued to rely on commodity exports?

6. What policies would be associated with import substitution industrialization?

7. What are the three stages of production in the ISI model?

8. What are the unintended consequences of ISI?

9. Why were exchange rates overvalued under ISI?

10. What were the benefits and costs of overvalued currencies?

11. What policies would be associated with ISI in Mexico?

12. Why were ISI policies abandoned in Latin America?

13. What created the economic crises of the 1980s?

14. Describe economic populism and the policies that would be associated with it.

15. What three conditions trigger economic populism?

16. Describe the cycle that results from economic populism.

17. What would the IMF do to stop the crisis caused by the policies of populists?

18. What external shocks did the economies of Latin America experience in the early 1980s?

19. What other factors combined with the external shocks to produce the debt crisis?

20. In 1987, it was clear that restoring capital flows to Latin America was not sufficient to deal with the region's problems. What three problems were observed that led to the conclusion that debt relief was necessary?

21. What was required under the Brady Plan?

22. What type of capital flow returned to Latin America after 1989?

138 Gerber • *International Economics*, Second Edition

23. What is the most lasting effect of the 1980s crisis?
    _____

24. What three types of reforms were undertaken?
    _____

25. What is recommended under the orthodox model? What additional policies does the heterodox model recommend?
    _____

26. What were the three main goals of trade reform?
    _____

27. What are the five macroeconomic components of the Washington Consensus?
    _____

28. What are the five microeconomic components of the Washington Consensus?
    _____

29. What problems continue to plague the Latin American region?
    _____

■ Just the Facts

1. Latin America is home to more than _____ million people, which is (greater than, less than, equal to) the population of the NAFTA region or the EU region.

2. The four countries of _____, _____, _____ and _____ account for the majority of population and economic activity in Latin America. Taken together, they account for _____ percent of the population of Latin America and _____ percent of the GNP.

3. _____ triggered a major shift in economic policy throughout Latin America.

4. Import substitution industrialization became the consensus theory of the economic development in the (1940s, 1950s, 1960s, 1980s, 1990s).

5. ISI favored (urban, rural) areas and hurt the _____ sector in particular.

6. Raul Prebisch worked for (the IMF, the United Nations, the WTO), and from there influenced economic policies across Latin America.

7. From 1950 to 1970, Mexican real GDP per capita grew at a rate of _____ percent per year, and manufacturing expanded from _____ percent of GDP to _____ percent.

8. In the cycle of economic populism experienced in Peru, GDP growth and real wage growth peaked in _____, inflation reached _____ percent, and real wages were (higher, lower, about the same) in 1990 as they were in 1985.

9. In _____ Mexico announced that it lacked the international reserves it needed to pay the interest and principle due on its foreign debt, thus beginning the Lost Decade.

10. Long term publicly guaranteed debt in Latin America and the Caribbean rose from slightly over _____ billion in 1973 to _____ billion in 1983.

11. In 1983, between _____ and _____ percent of the revenue earned by exports went to pay interest and was unavailable for investment or to purchase imports.

12. Between 1982 and 1986, the average rate of growth of real per capita GDP was _____ percent per year in Latin America and the Caribbean.

13. The Baker Plan tried to restart capital flows to Latin America through _____.

■ Review Quiz

Check your mastery of the chapter by selecting the letter that gives the correct answer to each question.

1. Which of the following is true?
   (a) The 1980s were a strong growth period for all but the most highly indebted Latin American countries.
   (b) Latin America has been consistently unable to produce economic growth and rising living standards.
   (c) For long stretches of the 20th century, Latin America was one of the fastest-growing regions in the world.
   (d) The Lost Decade did not change any of the prevailing economic policies in Latin America.

2. Common themes in Latin American countries include
   (a) independence movements that happened in the 19th century.
   (b) national identities of Latin American nations that are shallower than in other parts of the world.
   (c) an early period of industrialization in the late 19th and early 20th centuries.
   (d) all nations share the Spanish language and legacies of Spanish colonization.

3. Which of the following is false?
   (a) ISI advocates often overestimated the technical ability of government officials to identify market failures and their solutions.
   (b) ISI policies did not have problems with corruption and influence by a few elites.
   (c) When policies are heavily influenced by politics, special provisions, favors and economic inefficiencies tend to build up over time.
   (d) Powerful interest groups were able to use ISI policies to their own ends rather than in the national interest.

4. Raul Prebisch believed
   (a) the prices of raw materials were declining relative to price of manufactured goods.
   (b) the terms of trade for Latin American commodities would not decline due to increases in manufacturing productivity.
   (c) the demand for commodities would rise faster than the demand for manufactured goods.
   (d) a country should not import any products.

5. ISI policies
   (a) favored rural areas over urban areas.
   (b) increased economic equality because there were no favored elites.
   (c) led to overvalued exchange rates.
   (d) favored competition and forced firms to be efficient to survive.

6. After decades of ISI policies
   (a) Latin America continued to have the highest levels of income inequality of any region of the world.
   (b) infrastructure in rural areas improved relative to urban infrastructure.
   (c) domestic industry was more competitive because of the capital investment that took place.
   (d) Latin America no longer produced primary commodities for export.

7. Which of the following would not be a statement associated with Mexican ISI policies?
   (a) Economic policy is needed to meet the country's need for economic growth and fairer distribution of national income.
   (b) The government budget should be used to help targeted industries get access to investment funds.
   (c) Foreign investment should be limited and performance requirements used to match imports to export earnings.
   (d) Government power should be limited to reduce the potential for corruption.

8. All of the following are policies associated with ISI in Mexico except
   (a) Mexican exporters were required to convert their foreign exchange earnings into pesos at a rate that made exporting more profitable.
   (b) the government sold foreign exchange at artificially low prices to targeted firms.
   (c) the government nationalized key industries and turned them into state run monopolies.
   (d) the government used loans and loan guarantees to help firms in targeted industries obtain capital.

9. Which of the following would not be associated with the Brady Plan?
   (a) IMF and other multilateral loans at below market rates
   (b) National governments delivering on promises of economic reform
   (c) Commercial banks restructuring old loans and making new ones
   (d) Wage and price freezes

10. An orthodox model for controlling inflation would not include
    (a) freezing wages and prices.
    (b) reducing government spending.
    (c) increasing tax collection and compliance.
    (d) limits on the creation of new money.

11. Which of the following is true?
    (a) Stabilization policies might include deregulation of industry.
    (b) Structural reform policies might include reducing government budget deficits.
    (c) Structural reform policies might require privatizing government-owned industries.
    (d) Stabilization policies might address reducing trade barriers.

12. Trade reform in Latin America has not been successful at
    (a) increasing exports.
    (b) reducing quotas and non tariff barriers to trade.
    (c) increasing productivity.
    (d) reducing poverty and inequality.

■ Answers to Vocabulary

1. neoliberalism
2. Washington Consensus
3. orthodox stabilization policy
4. structural reform policies
5. Baker plan
6. heterodox stabilization policy
7. Lost Decade
8. Brady plan
9. populism
10. economic populism
11. import substitution industrialization (ISI)
12. market failure
13. Economic Commission on Latin America (ECLA, or CEPAL in Spanish)
14. terms of trade (TOT)
15. export pessimism

■ Answers to Chapter Review

1. Historical background including colonization, language, indigenous heritages, and independence movements that happened in the 19th century; economic policies in the 20th century that shifted from an outward, export oriented economy to an inward, targeted industry strategy; heavy levels of borrowing and indebtedness led to policy reforms in the region.

2. For long periods, it experienced some of the fastest growth in the world, but in the 1980s the entire region experienced negative per capita growth.

3. They were based on exports of agricultural commodities and minerals, with these sectors funded and controlled by foreign capital or a very small part of the domestic population. There were few linkages to the domestic economy and wealth was highly concentrated in the hands of just a few.

4. World War I disrupted trade and there was a particularly large drop in demand for export commodities and falling prices during the Depression. Demand and prices picked up during World War II but fell when the war was over.

5. Prebisch offered evidence of a long-run decline in the prices of raw materials relative to the prices of manufactured goods. The ratio of average export prices to average import prices is the terms of trade. At that time, the trend in the data for raw materials showed declining prices. Economic theory suggested that as incomes rose people spent smaller and smaller proportions of their income on food and other raw material based goods and more on manufactured items, meaning that the demand for primary commodities would decline relative to the demand for manufactured goods.

6. Replacing imported manufactured goods with domestically produced products is the basis of import substitution. Tariffs and other trade restrictions were used, the government created or supported new industrial development, and in general the policies were aimed at reducing the need for foreign exchange earnings.

7. The nation begins by developing manufacturing of simple consumer items. Next, intermediate industrial goods and more complex consumer goods are produced. The final state would have the nation producing complex industrial goods.

8. Governments misallocate resources when they become too involved in the production process. Exchange rates were often overvalued. The policies favored urban over rural areas. Inequality often worsened. There was widespread rent seeking activity.

9. Sometimes by deliberate government policy, but often because fixed exchange rates were used and inflation was higher than that of trading partners.

10. Overvalued exchange rates made it easier for targeted industries to buy imported capital goods and kept urban workers more allied with political leaders because foreign goods were relatively less expensive. It made it difficult to export, especially for the traditional commodity producers, which hurt investment and income in rural areas. Non-targeted industries lost sales and production. Industrial investment was too capital intensive and unable to create jobs fast enough to absorb labor leaving rural areas.

11. Strong, powerful government that owns and operates nationalized industries. Loans and loan guarantees, subsidized foreign exchange and other help for targeted industries to make capital investment easier. Export firms have to sell foreign exchange earnings at a lower peso price. Foreign investment is restricted.

12. They were unable to resolve the crises experienced in the 1980s and there was a growing perception that they were creating long-term economic inefficiencies.

13. faulty or misguided macroeconomic policies

14. A political movement that uses economic policies to attract votes from large groups, such as gaining the support of labor or domestically oriented businesses; strongly nationalistic and focused on economic growth and income re-distribution; relies on expansionary fiscal and monetary policies without regard for inflation, budget deficits, or foreign exchange constraints.

15. Dissatisfaction with current economic conditions; policy maker rejects traditional constraints on macro policy; policy maker raises wages while freezing prices and restructures the economy so that more products are produced domestically and there is less need for foreign exchange

16. Initially things improve because of the economic stimulus; bottlenecks emerge and lead to inflation, massive capital flight occurs as people fear a devaluation, and investment and wages fall. Often real wages are lower than before cycle started.

17. To stop the high inflation and balance of payments crisis, the IMF would oversee stabilization and structural reform policies that include budget cuts, slowdown in monetary growth, reduced trade barriers, and less government intervention.

18. the 1981 collapse of oil prices, increase in world interest rates, deep recession in the world's industrial economies that reduced demand and prices for raw materials

19. An acceleration in international lending had occurred from 1974 to 1982, macroeconomic mismanagement in the national economies of Latin America.

20. National aggregate expenditure was greater than national income; governments were printing money and creating high and persistent inflation; paying the debt itself left insufficient funds for domestic investment and consumption.

21. Lenders restructured some old debt into long-term, lower rate loans and made some new loans. The IMF made additional loans on concessional terms. Borrowing nations were required to demonstrate commitment to reform before getting new loans.

22. private capital flows in the form of both direct and portfolio investment

23. the deep economic reforms that mark a shift from protectionist, interventionist policies toward more open and market-oriented policies

24. Governments implemented stabilization plans to deal with inflation and budget deficits. Countries began privatizing government-owned industries. Trade policies became more open and less discriminatory toward exports.

25. The orthodox model calls for reduced government spending, reforming the tax system to increase compliance and revenue, and limitations on the creation of new money. The heterodox model adds wage and price freezes to eliminate inflationary expectations.

26. reduce the anti-export bias, raise productivity growth rate, lower real cost to consumers of traded goods

27. avoid large budget deficits, spend public money on health, education and basic services rather than on huge projects and special interests; cut taxes but tax a wide range of activities effectively; have interest rates higher than inflation with no preferential rates; make exchange rate competitive and credible

28. use tariffs not quotas and reduce them gradually; encourage foreign direct investment; privatize state enterprises where the market works; eliminate barriers and restrictions to competition; guarantee secure property rights

29. inadequate growth rates, dramatic inequality, and vulnerability to macroeconomic crises and volatility

■ Answers to Just the Facts

1. 500; greater than
2. Brazil; Mexico; Colombia; Argentina; 67; 75
3. The crises of the 1980s
4. 1950s
5. urban; agricultural
6. the United Nations
7. 3.1; 21.5; 29.4
8. 1986; 7,482; lower
9. August 1982

10. $37; $261
11. 10; 63
12. −1.8
13. renewed commercial bank lending

■ Answers to Review Quiz

1. C
2. A
3. B
4. A
5. C
6. A
7. D
8. A
9. D
10. A
11. C
12. D

Chapter 16
Export-Oriented Growth in East Asia

■ Vocabulary

For each numbered description, write in the correct term from the list provided.

deliberation council
demographic transition
Four Tigers

high-performance Asian economy (HPAE)
keiretsu

newly industrializing economy (NIE)
total factor productivity (TFP)

1. The share of labor productivity that is not explained by capital or education _____

2. The shift from high birth rates and high death rates to low birth rates and low death rates that accompanies modernization _____

3. One of the following economies, Hong Kong, Indonesia, Japan, Malaysia, Singapore, South Korea, Taiwan, and Thailand, which all share a number of economic policies, including outward orientation and rapid growth by world standards _____

4. Hong Kong, Singapore, S. Korea, and Taiwan, which all began their rapid economic growth in the 1950s and are now classified as high-income nations by the World Bank _____

5. One of a number of economies around the world that began high rates of economic growth after the take-off of the Four Tigers _____

6. A quasi-legislative body that brings together representatives from the private and public sector _____

7. Japanese organizational structure where firms are legally separate entities but are tied to each other through their ownership structure, business relations, and inter-locking directorates _____

■ Chapter Review

Answer the questions in the space provided below each.

1. What common characteristics do the high performance Asian economies (HPAE) share?

2. What do economists agree are the keys to the growth of the HPAEs?

3. What questions remain about the HPAEs policies?

4. What is the biggest contrast between the HPAEs and the Latin American region?

5. What mechanisms did the HPAEs use to share wealth across all layers of society?

6. How do the policies described above create positive effects across society?

7. How were the HPAEs able to rapidly accumulate physical and human capital?

8. Describe the "virtuous cycle."

9. How did educational policy in the HPAEs affect growth rates?

10. Besides education, what policies did Japan and the Four Tigers use that were helpful in promoting exports?

11. What were the key differences in the HPAEs in terms of both avoiding and surviving macroeconomic crises?

12. What components of the institutional environment in the HPAEs are critical?

13. Except for Japan, in what area do the HPAEs compare poorly with the United States and Western Europe?

14. How are interdependent investment activities coordinated in the HPAEs? What benefits does this offer?

15. What is remarkable about the interventionist government policies of the HPAEs compared to the experience of other nations?

16. What explanation do economists offer for this?

17. What are the distinguishing features of keiretsu?

18. In what areas did the World Bank conclude that government intervention was common in the HPAEs?

19. What tools did nations use to promote specific industries?

20. How were the HPAE attempts at targeting specific industries different than those of other nations?

21. How did directed credit programs contribute to the Asian financial crisis?

22. How might exports create benefits for the economy that are different from domestically produced products?

23. How do GATT rules effect other nations that might want to follow the HPAE model?

24. What do studies of total factor productivity conclude about the HPAE growth story?

■ Just the Facts

1. The eight economies that make up the high performance Asian economies or HPAEs include _____, _____, _____, _____, _____, _____, _____, and _____.

2. The countries worst hit by the Asian financial crisis include _____, _____, _____, and _____.

3. By 2000, all the countries worst hit by the financial crisis had returned to positive growth in the range of _____ to _____ percent in real terms.

4. The Four Tigers include _____, _____, _____, and _____.

5. _____ began rapid growth in the 1950s, followed by _____. The _____ began their high rates of economic growth later.

6. Income levels in the HPAEs are (higher, lower, similar to) income levels in Latin America.

7. Between 1960 and 1980, real GDP per capita in Singapore increased more than _____ percent.

8. In the HPAEs, the richest 20 percent of households receives incomes that are on average _____ times higher than the poorest 20 percent of households, while in Latin America, the richest 20 percent of households receives income an average of almost _____ times higher than the poorest 20 percent.

9. Investment in education in the HPAEs was focused on the _____ level.

10. Japan began the shift from ISI policies to export promotion in the _____, the Four Tigers switched in the _____, and the NIEs switched in the _____.

11. Between 1965 and 2000, the HPAEs had more than a _____ percent increase in their share of total world exports and total world manufactured exports.

12. Many of the most prominent and best known Japanese firms are organized into _____, and the six largest include about _____ of the 200 largest Japanese companies and account for about _____ percent of all sales in Japan.

13. The overall rate of foreign direct investment is (higher, lower, similar) in Japan than in other countries.

14. _____ appears to have been one of the major causes of the Asian financial crisis.

15. Developing countries were responsible for nearly _____ percent of world merchandise exports in 2002, a figure that has been relatively stable over a long period of time.

16. Between 1966 and 1985, Singapore raised investment from _____ percent of GDP to _____ percent.

17. The key to the outstanding growth in the HPAEs appears to be _____.

■ Review Quiz

Check your mastery of the chapter by selecting the letter that gives the correct answer to each question.

1. Which of the following is not a key factor contributing to the success of the HPAEs?
    (a) Macroeconomic stability
    (b) Government spending on education, health care, and infrastructure
    (c) Openness to imports, especially of capital goods
    (d) Democratic and open societies

2. Which of the following government industrial policies proved the most problematic in the Asian financial crisis?
    (a) Deliberation councils
    (b) Export subsidies
    (c) Directed credit
    (d) Free public education

3. More saving today in an economy leads to all of the following except:
    (a) More investment
    (b) More rapid capital accumulation
    (c) Increases in national income
    (d) Future decreases in saving as goals are realized

4. Which of the following is not one of the Four Tigers?
   (a) Japan
   (b) South Korea
   (c) Hong Kong
   (d) Singapore

5. The HPAEs used all of the following mechanisms to ensure growth was shared across income levels except
   (a) free public education.
   (b) land reform.
   (c) spending on rural infrastructure.
   (d) deliberation councils.

6. Which of the following is not a key difference between the experience of the HPAEs and Latin America?
   (a) Incomes are more equally distributed in the HPAEs than in Latin America.
   (b) Budget deficits and foreign debts were kept more proportional to income and to economic growth in the HPAEs than in Latin America.
   (c) Less rent seeking occurred in the HPAEs than in Latin America.
   (d) Throughout the 20th century, growth was more rapid in the HPAEs than in Latin America.

7. The 1980s in the HPAEs was a time of
   (a) strong and sometimes accelerating growth.
   (b) slow growth.
   (c) no growth.
   (d) recession/depression.

8. Which of the following is true?
   (a) Deliberation councils offer firms the chance to individually meet in private with bureaucrats.
   (b) Bureaucrats tend to be highly educated, respected, and well paid in the HPAEs and are relatively isolated from political pressures.
   (c) Firms that received assistance through government industrial policies faced no performance requirements.
   (d) There is not much society-wide buy in to the notion of having economic growth create benefits across society.

9. Recent studies have concluded
   (a) the growth model practiced by the HPAEs is entirely new.
   (b) industrial policies in the HPAEs account for most of the growth that occurred in the region.
   (c) capital and education account for most of the growth in the region.
   (d) savings and investment were not critical for the HPAEs.

10. Which of the following is false?
    (a) Exports can be good for a nation because they create revenue that allows imports of new technology and capital equipment that may not be able to be produced at home.
    (b) Countries that export can take advantage of economies of scale to lower production costs and improve efficiency.
    (c) Exports reduce competitive pressures on domestic firms.
    (d) Exports may speed up the adoption of international best practices.

■ Answers to Vocabulary

1. total factor productivity (TFP)
2. demographic transition
3. high-performance Asian economy (HPAE)
4. Four Tigers
5. newly industrializing economy (NIE)
6. deliberation council
7. keiretsu

■ Answers to Chapter Review

1. an outward orientation and rapid growth by world standards
2. macroeconomic stability has been a high priority of their economic policies, strong, and credible commitments to sharing economic growth across all layers of society; exports have been promoted while being more open to imports than other developing countries
3. how important have industrial policies been to their growth; have the government interventionist polices in the region avoided the rent seeking behavior observed in Latin America, and if so, how; does their growth represent a new model
4. growth continued and even accelerated in the HPAEs in the 1980s
5. land reform, free public education, free basic health care, significant investments in rural infrastructure, such as clean water, transportation, and communication systems
6. With purchasing power spread across society, small- and medium-sized enterprises develop to serve local markets and can gain experience and grow. Rising incomes raise hope for future improvements and encourage cooperation and legitimacy for the government. This leads to political stability and can encourage business elites to make long-term investments.
7. High levels of investment require high levels of savings. The proportion of their population working was higher due to the demographic transition, high inflation was absent, and stable financial institutions were present, all of which encouraged saving. With rapid income growth, savings rise.
8. Income growth leads to more savings, which leads to high rates of investment, rapid income growth, and more savings, investment, and income growth.
9. Spending was focused on the primary and secondary level, where it has greater social impact. Literacy rates rose dramatically and laid the foundation for a skilled labor force. As the educational level rose, workers could take on more technological, sophisticated production, pushing new investment into new product lines.

10. made export financing credit readily available, required export targets for firms that wished to receive favorable credit terms or tax benefits; provided tariff-free access to imports of capital equipment used to manufacture exports

11. Budget deficits and foreign debts remained at generally manageable levels. Governments were committed to low inflation and that helps avoid severe real appreciations in the exchange rate. Differences between the real exchange rate, the real interest rate, and the inflation rate were relatively low, fostering greater security in the minds of investors.

12. Property rights are relatively secure and free from the threat of nationalization. Bureaucracies are generally competent, contracts are enforceable, access to information is widespread, and regulations are clear and well publicized.

13. political rights and civil liberties

14. Six of the eight use deliberation councils with representatives from both the private and public sectors. They reduce the costs of acquiring information, allow for bargaining over policies, give greater investor confidence, raise credibility for government policies, and give the business elite a strong voice, and thus cooperation, with the overall strategy.

15. the lack of rent seeking activities

16. The use of deliberation councils has the business community interacting with the government as a group rather than individually; performance requirements tied to anything businesses did receive of value, with the requirements being more enforceable than in other regions; bureaucrats that are highly educated, respected, and well paid and that are more insulated from the political process; the overall commitment to shared growth.

17. cross-ownership of firms; interlocking directorates; management jointly plan economic strategies and meet regularly to discuss business conditions and practices; control over distribution channels

18. targeted specific industries, directed credit, and export promotion

19. restrictions on imports, export subsidies, directed credit, market information, infrastructure construction, research and development funds

20. Resources were tied to specific export targets and were withdrawn if the target wasn't met. Governments placed macroeconomic stability over industrial policies.

21. Government involvement forced banks to make unsound loans. Failure to apply normal lending criteria led to a mountain of bad debt, which caused many banks to fail and put the whole financial sector in jeopardy.

22. Because they produce for a larger market, economies of scale may come into play, there are added incentives to undertake research and development, firms may more quickly adopt international best practices and are forced to be highly competitive. Export earnings make possible the purchase of imports, which could include capital and technological products the domestic economy is not capable of producing.

23. Credit subsidies, tax breaks, and direct payments to targeted industries are no longer allowed. Subsidies contingent on export performance are not allowed.

24. The vast majority of growth can be accounted for by the high rates of education and capital formation and not by other factors that could include industrial policies.

■ Answers to Just the Facts

1. Hong Kong; Indonesia; Japan; Malaysia; Singapore; South Korea; Taiwan; Thailand
2. Indonesia; Malaysia; South Korea; Thailand
3. 5; 10
4. Hong Kong; Singapore; South Korea, and Taiwan
5. Japan; the Four Tigers; newly industrializing economies (NIEs)
6. higher
7. 400
8. 6.7; 18
9. primary and secondary
10. 1950s; 1960s; 1980s
11. 200
12. keiretsu; one half; 15
13. lower
14. Government directed credit programs
15. 26
16. 11; 40
17. high rates of saving and investment

■ Answers to Review Quiz

1. D
2. C
3. D
4. A
5. D
6. D
7. A
8. B
9. C
10. C

Chapter 17
Economic Integration in the Transition Economies

■ Vocabulary

For each numbered description, write in the correct term from the list provided.

accession protocol
centrally planned economy
Central and East European (CEE) countries
Central European Free Trade Agreement (CEFTA)
Council for Mutual Economic Assistance (CMEA or COMECON)
counter-trade
counter-purchase trade
currency convertibility
Europe Agreements
monetary overhang
newly independent states (NIS) of the former Soviet Union
Partnership and Cooperation Agreements (PCAs)
special economic zone (SEZ)
swap rate
transition economy

1. Any economy that is undergoing a transition from socialism to capitalism or from a command economy to a market economy _____

2. Poland, Czech Republic, Slovakia, Hungary, Slovenia, Croatia, Bosnia Herzegovina, Yugoslavia, Albania, Macedonia, Bulgaria, Latvia, Lithuania, Estonia _____

3. An economy where the fundamental decisions about what to produce, how to produce it, and who gets it, are made by a central authority and markets have little or no role in allocative decisions _____

4. A more market-oriented developmental area/region in China that is set up to experiment with new forms of economic organizations and to develop joint ventures by attracting foreign investment _____

5. A Soviet organization of economic cooperation within its sphere of power _____

6. Armenia, Azerbaijan, Georgia, Kazakhstan, Kyrgyz Republic, Tajikistan, Turkmenistan, Uzbekistan, Belarus, Moldova, Ukraine _____

7. A form of barter for nations that did not have currencies that were freely convertible _____

8. An exporting country is required to spend its earnings on imports of equal value from the country receiving its exports, always maintaining balanced trade _____

9. The rate at which two monetary authorities settled claims on each other _____

154 Gerber • *International Economics*, Second Edition

10. The right to freely purchase currencies at the official, unified exchange rate _____

11. Also know as liquidity overhang, this is the accumulation of a large amount of unspent domestic currency because consumers cannot find the goods and services they want to buy
    _____

12. An asymmetric trade opening where the EU lowed its barriers to the Central and East European countries more quickly than those nations lowered their barriers to EU products
    _____

13. Agreements between the European Union and the Newly Independent States, giving the NIS countries access to the EU market through the GATT/WTO framework by granting them MFN status
    _____

14. The set of steps new members must take in order to put their policies in compliance with the rules of the WTO _____

15. Free trade agreement between Poland, Czech Republic, Slovak Republic, Hungary, Romania, and Slovenia _____

■ Chapter Review

Answer the questions in the space provided below each.

1. What tasks do the transition economies share to successfully transition to market-based economies?
   _____

2. How are economic decisions made in a centrally planned economy?
   _____

3. In what three ways do centrally planned economies differ from market economies?
   _____

4. What was the promise of central planning?
   _____

5. What were positive results of central planning?
   _____

6. What were negative results of central planning?
   _____

7. What are some of the core problems with central planning?
   _____

8. How did international trade work under central planning?
   _____

9. Why does a steep depression result in the early stages of the transition from centrally planning to markets?

10. What is reform fatigue?

11. What are the features of economic stabilization in the transition economies?

12. What problems faced government budgets in the transition economies?

13. What did most transition governments do to deal with their budget problems?

14. What does liberalization involve? Give examples of what is required.

15. Which approach (gradual or fast) to the transition seems to be supported by empirical measures?

16. What does more recent research indicate were the three causes of depression in the transition economies?

17. What are two remarkable shifts in the transition economies?

18. If currencies are not convertible, how is trade completed?

19. What did the CEE substitute for trade with the CMEA nations?

20. What barriers to trade continue to be important in the CEE countries?

21. What are the three steps to trade liberalization in the transition economies?

22. What is the major factor in explaining China's phenomenal export growth?

23. Why are import surges common in the early stages of the reform process?

156 Gerber • *International Economics,* Second Edition

24. Beyond import surges, what three factors compound the problem of trade balances in the early stages of the transition?

25. What makes it difficult for transition economies to maintain a devalued exchange rate?

26. What tasks must be accomplished in transition economies regarding foreign exchange markets?

27. How did monetary overhang complicate the introduction of foreign exchange convertibility?

28. What are the key requirements for membership in the WTO?

29. What are the advantages of membership in the WTO for the transition economies?

30. What are the barriers to NIS countries joining the European Union?

31. What were the three major issues in debate over China's entry into the WTO?

32. U.S. bilateral negotiations with China for its entry into the WTO focused on which six issues?

■ Just the Facts

1. In May 2004, _____ of the Central and Eastern European countries and _____ of the former Soviet countries joined the European Union, meaning they are well on their way to establishing market economies and democratic governments.

2. All countries are moving away from _____ for their economies.

3. Under central planning, most enterprises are _____.

4. With the exception of the new EU entrants, all the transition economies fall into the World Bank classification of _____ nations.

5. The Visegrad Four include the nations of _____, _____, _____, and _____.

6. _____ was the first nation to begin market reforms and began implementing them in _____.

7. _____ continues to hold back reform efforts in many former centrally planned economies.

8. After the break up of the Soviet Union, all of the countries experienced _____.

9. The (CEE, Baltics, NIS) began to recover first after the break up of the Soviet Union.

10. Five of the NIS and one Baltic Republic saw their GDP decline more than _____ percent.

11. In 2002, _____, _____, _____, and _____ were still operating at levels more than 50 percent below their pre-transition levels.

12. _____, _____, _____, _____ and _____ all had GDP levels in 2002 that were more than 100 percent of their pre-transition output.

13. In the early years of the transition, _____ rose rapidly.

14. _____ is a model of slow reform.

15. _____ is a model for rapid transition or the "big bang" approach.

16. Balance of payment problems were (common, relatively rare, not possible) in the centrally planned economies prior to the transition.

17. Over the last two decades, the Chinese national economy grew nearly _____ percent per year and exports grew _____ percent. By 2000, China was the _____ largest exporter in the world and the _____ largest recipient of foreign investment.

18. Most transitional economies begin their stabilization and transition programs with _____ of their domestic currency.

19. All of the transition economies except _____ are in the WTO or have observer status.

20. Between 1992 and 2002, China received nearly _____ of all foreign direct investment into developing countries.

21. In 2002, China supplied _____ percent of the world's exports and purchased _____ percent of the world's imports.

■ Review Quiz

Check your mastery of the chapter by selecting the letter that gives the correct answer to each question.

1. Which of the following is false?
   (a) The transition economies are located in Central and Eastern Europe and Asia.
   (b) All the transition economies are well on their way to completing the transition to market economies.
   (c) Accurately measuring output in the transition economies is often challenging.
   (d) Some transition economies have risen above the lower-middle income World Bank classification.

2. When did the transition to market economies begin?
   (a) China began implementing gradual reforms in 1979.
   (b) When the Soviet Union collapsed
   (c) When the Berlin Wall fell
   (d) Around 1990

3. Every country in Central and Eastern Europe experienced _____ at the beginning of the reform process.
   (a) a deep recession
   (b) an overvalued currency
   (c) a current account surplus
   (d) labor shortages

4. The nations that were fastest to improve after the collapse of the Soviet Union were
   (a) the CEE.
   (b) the Baltics.
   (c) the NIS.
   (d) the Russian federation.

5. Which of the following does not describe one of the four tasks that must be completed in the transition?
   (a) Implementing economic stabilization policies
   (b) Restricting the inflow of foreign capital
   (c) Defining property rights
   (d) Developing institutions

6. World trade in the transition economies
   (a) has grown, but with the same trade partners as before the transition.
   (b) has declined.
   (c) has grown overall, but with different partners than before the transition.
   (d) has not changed overall, but the partners have changed.

7. Which of the following is false?
   (a) The transition to a market economy has proceeded relatively successfully and at a slow, gradual pace for the Chinese economy.
   (b) The transition to a market economy has been rapid in Vietnam and has been largely successful.
   (c) Slow and gradual transitions are not supported by the empirical data regarding the best approach to adopt.
   (d) Data from the World Bank show a smaller average decline in GDP and a quicker return to growth for countries that were slow, gradual reformers.

8. Under the centrally planned economies,
   (a) no international trade took place.
   (b) trade was carefully coordinated so that no currency had to change hands.
   (c) nations traded only rarely and only with industrial economies that produced capital goods they could otherwise not obtain.
   (d) firms were free to trade with whomever they wanted as long as they paid or received cash.

9. Which of the following is not a step toward trade liberalization in transition economies?
   (a) Create government monopolies to jump start trade
   (b) Allow domestic prices to be linked to world prices
   (c) Develop explicit trade policy rules
   (d) Decide which forms of protection are necessary and which products to protect

10. In the CEE countries during the transition,
    (a) trade reform was slow and gradual.
    (b) quantitative restrictions on imports and nontariff barriers were heavily utilized.
    (c) WTO membership was not a significant strategy.
    (d) tariff rates were set at fairly low levels.

11. Which of the following is false?
    (a) Most of the transitional economies began their transition and stabilization programs with large devaluations.
    (b) Devaluations are preferred to tariffs as a way to protect the balance of payments.
    (c) Devaluations create an incentive to export.
    (d) Devaluations create a protective wall around selected industries that allow domestic producers to delay their adjustment to world prices and perpetuates the misallocation of resources.

12. Monetary overhang
    (a) is reduced if the currency is overvalued.
    (b) can make the conversion to a convertible exchange rate fail.
    (c) does not affect the nation's need for foreign exchange reserves.
    (d) reduces the need for foreign exchange reserves by the nation.

13. Import surges do all of the following except
    (a) hurt consumer well being.
    (b) help firms obtain necessary capital goods.
    (c) lead to large trade deficits and potential balance of payments problems.
    (d) require capital inflows to finance.

■ Answers to Vocabulary

1. transition economy
2. Central and East European (CEE) countries
3. centrally planned economy
4. special economic zone (SEZ)
5. Council for Mutual Economic Assistance (CMEA or COMECON)
6. newly independent states (NIS) of the former Soviet Union
7. counter-trade
8. counter-purchase trade
9. swap rate
10. currency convertibility
11. monetary overhang
12. Europe Agreements
13. Partnership and Cooperation Agreements (PCAs)
14. accession protocol
15. Central European Free Trade Agreement (CEFTA)

Answers to Chapter Review

1. Macroeconomic policies must strive for stability. Domestic prices must be linked to world prices. Labor markets and financial markets must be created. Property rights must be defined and become enforceable. Institutional structures to support markets must be developed.

2. The fundamental decisions of what to produce, how to produce it, and how to distribute it are made by a central planning authority. They use mathematical models to set output targets for each industry. Markets have little or no role in allocating resources.

3. Production, prices, and trade are all controlled by the central planning authority. There are no asset markets. There are not labor markets in the normal sense–wages are set and workers are allocated by central planners and dismissals are not allowed.

4. That it could free society from the volatility and uncertainty of markets through conscious control over economic development, that incomes could be more equally distributed, and that basic necessities could be economic rights for citizens.

5. Unemployment was low, income distribution was relatively more equal, and education and health care were high relative to income levels.

6. Everything depended on the coercive power of the state to create forced savings. Economies became more distorted over time. Heavy industry was favored over other types of production. Many manufacturing industries wound up producing negative value added, with the value of inputs greater than the value of the output. The cumulation of inefficiencies negatively impacted economic growth.

7. It does not provide incentives for efficiency or innovation. It requires an authoritarian political system to enforce the dictates of the plan, which in practice led to creation of powerful political elites.

8. Trade was limited and controlled by the planning authority and largely limited to other centrally planned economies. Most trade with them is by barter. Products sold on the world market for foreign exchange are used to import products that cannot be obtained elsewhere.

9. The central planning authority stops allocating resources. Uncertainty about where the economy will go leads many industries to set idle, especially the most inefficient and uncompetitive. Negative growth continues until enough of the new economy outweighs the disappearance of the old economy.

10. Countries become exhausted from the loss of income and the additional uncertainty and have slowed or partially reversed their transitions.

11. controlling inflation, budget deficits, and external debt to stabilize the macroeconomy

12. Heavy industries required massive subsidies and shutting them down completely meant large spending on social programs. Tax systems were not developed. There were no financial markets for borrowing.

13. a combination of printing money and borrowing internationally from multilateral lending agencies

14. the replacement of administrative controls with market-based allocative mechanisms; freeing domestic prices, firms hiring and production decisions, opening export and import markets, removing barriers to entry

15. The more consistent and rapid the reform policies, data suggests, the quicker the return to growth

16. the disruption of traditional trading patterns, the shift in internal demand from state-produced goods to the small consumer goods sector; and disruptions in input supply

17. the change in trading patterns and the growth of trade generally

18. Imports from a nation are matched with exports to that nation so no currency changes hands.

19. new trade with high-income, industrial countries
20. lack of domestic infrastructure, such as telecommunications and border-crossing facilities; insufficient information about foreign markets; inconsistent or unclear government regulations
21. Remove barriers to entry in the trade sector, link domestic prices to world prices, and formulate an explicit trade policy.
22. Reforms shifted production toward China's comparative advantage and firms must be more responsive to world prices and profitability.
23. There is excess demand for consumer products, and the modernization of infrastructure and production require imported technology and capital goods.
24. Most countries implement stabilization policies that make it difficult for firms to obtain bank credit for exports. Trade collapses with former centrally planned partners and demand decreases due to the stabilization policies. The lag in institutional development creates uncertainty that makes it difficult to export.
25. higher rates of inflation
26. Exchange rates must be unified, an exchange rate system must be chosen and individuals and enterprises must be granted the right to freely purchase foreign currencies at the official, unified exchange rate.
27. Households accumulated large holdings of unspent domestic currency. There are not sufficient inflows or stocks of foreign exchange to meet the demand from domestic currency holders.
28. transparency in the trade regime, compliance with WTO rules regarding tariffs and quotas, elimination of export subsidies and most direct production subsidies
29. guarantees of MFN status and low tariff rates for exported products; binding of tariffs, which reduces rent seeking by domestic producers; access to the dispute settlement process; a strong signal to the rest of the world that the nation's trade policies are acceptable; gives the nation a voice in establishing future trade rules
30. Most haven't advanced in their transition to market economies; many are not functioning democracies; most lack the administrative and technical capacity to implement and enforce EU rules; talk of membership upsets the balance of political power; and the nations are geographically isolated and have far deeper cultural ties to the Middle East than to Europe.
31. specific trade-related issues; issues of national security; issues of human rights
32. tariff reduction; elimination of nontariff barriers; service industry access to the Chinese market; protection of investment and intellectual property rights; safeguards for import surges and dumping cases; anti-competitive behavior of Chinese state-owned industry.

■ Answers to Just the Facts

1. 5; 3
2. central planning
3. state owned
4. low-income or lower-middle income
5. Czech Republic; Slovak Republic; Hungary; Poland
6. China; 1979

7. Politics
8. a deep recession
9. CEE
10. 50
11. Georgia; Moldova; Ukraine; Tajikistan
12. Poland; Czech Republic; Hungary; Slovak Republic; Slovenia
13. inflation
14. China
15. Vietnam
16. not possible
17. 10; 14; 4th; 2nd
18. large devaluations
19. Turkmenistan
20. one-fourth
21. 5; 4.5

■ Answers to Review Quiz

1. B
2. A
3. A
4. A
5. B
6. C
7. D
8. B
9. A
10. D
11. D
12. B
13. A